What Every Teacher Should Know About Classroom Management

James Levin
Pennsylvania State University

James F. Nolan
Pennsylvania State University

Boston   New York   San Francisco
Mexico City   Montreal   Toronto   London   Madrid   Munich   Paris
Hong Kong   Singapore   Tokyo   Cape Town   Sydney

TABLE OF CONTENTS

What Every Teacher Should Know About Classroom Management

I. FOUNDATIONS

Defining a Discipline Problem

Teachers often describe students who have discipline problems as lazy, unmotivated, belligerent, aggressive, angry, or argumentative. These words at best are imprecise, judgmental, and descriptive of a wide range of behaviors. After all, a student can be lazy or angry and yet not be a disruptive factor in the classroom. Furthermore, attribution theory (Weiner, 1980) tells us that our thoughts guide our feelings, which in turn guide our behavior. Therefore, when teachers describe children using negative labels, they are much more likely to feel and behave negatively toward those children (Brendtro et al., 1990). Negative teacher behavior is ineffective in helping children learn appropriate behavior. Thus, for a definition of a discipline problem to be useful to a teacher, it must clearly differentiate student behavior that requires immediate corrective action from that which does not.

The amount of material that has been written on discipline and classroom management is staggering. Hundreds of books and articles on this subject have been produced for both the professional and the general public, the great majority of them appearing since the mid-1970s. They typically cover such areas as the types and frequency of behavior problems, the causes of student misbehavior, and the strategies that teachers can employ to improve classroom management. However, surprisingly, the most basic question, "What types of student behaviors constitute discipline problems?" has rarely been considered. Having a clear understanding of what behaviors constitute discipline problems is a prerequisite for effective classroom management; without this understanding, it is impossible for teachers to design and communicate to students rational and meaningful classroom guidelines, to recognize misbehavior when it occurs, or to employ management strategies effectively and consistently.

In developing an operational definition, it is helpful to examine some infrequent definitions found in the literature. Kindsvatter (1978) defines discipline in terms of student behavior in the classroom, or "classroom decorum." He uses terms such as behavior problems and misbehavior but never gives meanings or examples for them. However, he does associate discipline with student behavior (which we will see does not always have to be the case).

Feldhusen (1978) uses the term disruptive behavior, which he defines as a violation of school expectations interfering with the orderly conduct of teaching. This definition is significant because it states that misbehavior is any student behavior that interferes with teaching. In defining disruptive behavior in this manner, Feldhusen attempts to provide teachers with a guideline for monitoring student behavior: Any behavior that keeps the teacher from teaching

1

is a disciplinary problem; any behavior that does not interrupt the teaching process is not a discipline problem.

Using this guideline, it seems relatively easy to identify discipline problems. Or is it? Let's test it by applying it to a number of common classroom behaviors: (1) a student continually calls out while the teacher is explaining material; (2) a student quietly scratches his name into his desk; and (3) a student quietly passes notes to his neighbor. According to Feldhusen's definition only the first student is exhibiting a discipline problem because his calling out interferes with the teacher's ability to teach. Unless a teacher were quite observant, the second and third behaviors could go unnoticed. Even if the teacher were aware of these behaviors, he could easily continue to teach. However, how many teachers would agree that scratching one's name on a desk and passing notes do not constitute discipline problems? Teachers realize inherently that such behaviors do constitute discipline problems and must be managed. Therefore, Feldhusen's definition is inadequate.

Emmer et al. (1989) offer a more comprehensive definition: "Student behavior is disruptive when it seriously interferes with the activities of the teacher or of several students for more than a brief time" (p. 187). Under this definition, disruptive behavior interferes not only with the teacher or teaching act but also with students or the learning act. This is an important enhancement because it recognizes the right of every student to learn (Bauer, 1985), and most of the time in a classroom the need of the group must override the need of an individual student (Curwin and Mendler, 1980).

Unfortunately the definition includes the terms seriously, several, and brief time. Although these terms are used to generalize to a wider range of situations, they allow room for disagreement and misinterpretation. First, a brief time or a serious interference for one teacher may not be a brief time or serious interruption for another. Second, is it only when several students are disrupted that a discipline problem exists? If we apply this definition to the three types of behaviors listed previously, the student who calls out and possibly the note passer would be identified. The student who is defacing the desk would not be covered.

By far one of the most comprehensive definitions has been offered by Shrigley (1979), who states that any behavior that disrupts the teaching act or is psychologically or physically unsafe constitutes a disruptive behavior. This definition includes behaviors that do not necessarily interfere with the teaching act but are definitely psychologically or physically unsafe, such as running in a science lab, unsafe use of tools or laboratory equipment, threats to other students, and constant teasing and harassing of classmates. However, the same problem is evident in this definition as in Feldhusen's: name-scratching and note-passing would not be considered discipline problems because they do not interfere with teaching and are not unsafe.

2

It should be clear from this discussion, that any definition of the term discipline problem must provide teachers with the means to determine instantly whether or not any given behavior is a discipline problem. Once this identification has been made, the teacher can then decide what specific teacher intervention should be employed.

Consider the following six scenarios. For each, ask yourself the following questions:

1. Is there a discipline problem?
2. If there is a discipline problem, who is exhibiting it?
3. Why is the behavior a discipline problem or why isn't the behavior a discipline problem?

Scenario 1: Marisa quietly enters the room and takes her seat. The teacher requests that students take out their homework. Marisa does not take out her homework but instead takes out a magazine and begins to flip quietly through the pages. The teacher ignores Marisa and involves the class in reviewing the homework.

Scenario 2: Marisa quietly enters the room and takes her seat. The teacher requests that students take out their homework. Marisa does not take out her homework but instead takes out a magazine and begins to flip quietly through the pages. The teacher publicly announces that there will be no review of the homework until Marisa puts away the magazine and takes out her homework.

Scenario 3: Marisa quietly enters the room and takes her seat. The teacher requests that students take out their homework. Marisa does not take out her homework but instead takes out a magazine and begins to flip quietly through the pages. The teacher begins to involve the class in reviewing the homework and at the same time moves closer to Marisa. The review continues with the teacher standing in close proximity to Marisa.

Scenario 4: Marisa quietly enters the room and takes her seat. The teacher requests that students take out their homework. Marisa does not take out her homework but instead takes out a magazine and begins to show the magazine to the students who sit next to her. The teacher ignores Marisa and begins to involve the class in the review of the homework. Marisa continues to show the magazine to her neighbors.

3

Scenario 5: Marisa quietly enters the room and takes her seat. The teacher requests that students take out their homework. Marisa does not take out her homework but instead takes out a magazine and begins to show the magazine to the students who sit next to her. The teacher does not begin the review and, in front of the class, loudly demands that Marisa put the magazine away and get out her homework. The teacher stares at Marisa for the two minutes that it takes her to put the magazine away and find her homework. Once Marisa finds her homework the teacher begins the review.

Scenario 6: Marisa quietly enters the room and takes her seat. The teacher requests that students take out their homework. Marisa does not take out her homework but instead takes out a magazine and begins to show the magazine to the students who sit next to her. The teacher begins the homework review and, at the same time, walks toward Marisa. While a student is answering a question the teacher, as privately as possible, assertively asks Marisa to take out her homework and put the magazine away.

    If you are like many of the teachers to whom we have given these same six scenarios you probably have found answering the questions that preceded them difficult. Furthermore, if you have taken time to discuss your answers with others, you undoubtedly have discovered your answers differ from theirs.

    Much of the difficulty in determining what constitutes a discipline problem can be avoided using the following definition, which recognizes that discipline problems are multifaceted: *A discipline problem is behavior that (1) interferes with the teaching act, (2) interferes with the rights of others to learn, (3) is psychologically or physically unsafe, or (4) destroys property.* This definition not only covers calling out, defacing property, or disturbing other students but also other common behaviors which teachers confront every day. Note, however, that the definition does not limit behavior to student behavior. This is very important, for it means the teacher must consider his own behavior as well as his students' behavior.

    Using our new definition, review the six scenarios again and compare your analysis with ours. In Scenario 1 there are no discipline problems because neither Marisa's nor the teacher's behavior is interfering with the rights of others to learn. The teacher has decided to ignore Marisa for the time being and focus on involving the class with the homework review.

    In Scenario 2 the teacher is a discipline problem because the teacher has interrupted the homework review to intervene with Marisa, who isn't interfering with any other students' learning. In this situation, it is the teacher who is interfering with the rights of the students to learn.

    In Scenario 3 there is no evident discipline problem. Neither Marisa's nor the teacher's behavior is interfering with the other students' right to learn.

The teacher has not decided to ignore Marisa but has wisely chosen an intervention strategy that allows the homework review to continue.

In Scenario 4 both Marisa and the teacher are discipline problems. Marisa is interfering with the other students' right to learn. Since Marisa is a discipline problem, by ignoring her, the teacher also interferes with the other students' right to learn.

In Scenario 5 Marisa and the teacher are again discipline problems. Marisa's sharing of the magazine is disruptive but the teacher's choice of intervention is also a problem. In fact, the teacher is interfering with the learning of more students than Marisa.

In Scenario 6 Marisa is still a discipline problem. However, the teacher is not because the intervention strategy allows him to work with the class and, at the same time, manage Marisa.

The guidelines provided by the definition make it far easier to determine whether or not a discipline problem exists, and if it does, who has the problem. Most nondiscipline problems can be managed at some later time, after the other students have begun their work, during a break, or before or after class. When a discipline problem is evident, however, the teacher must intervene immediately, because by definition there exists a behavior that is interfering with other students' rights or safety. When a teacher inappropriately or ineffectively employs management strategies that result in interference with the learning of others, he, in fact, becomes the discipline problem. Note that under the terms of the definition, inappropriate or ill-timed classroom procedures, public address announcements, and school policies that tend to disrupt the teaching and/or learning process are discipline problems.

Problem Student Behavior Outside the Definition

By now some readers have probably thought of many student behaviors that are not covered by our definition; for example, students who refuse to turn in homework, who are not prepared for class, or who are daydreaming, as well as the occasional student who gives the teacher "dirty looks." A careful analysis of these behaviors will reveal that under the terms of the definition, they are not discipline problems. They may be motivational problems.

Motivational problems can occur because of low levels of self-confidence, low expectations for success, lack of interest in academics, lost feelings of autonomy, achievement anxieties, or fears of success or failure (Stipek, 1998). Thus, working with students who have motivational problems often involves long-term individualized intervention and/or referrals to professionals outside the classroom.

Although in-depth coverage of motivational problems is beyond the scope of this book, it must be recognized that some strategies used to manage these problems, which generally do not interfere with other students' learning,

5

disturb the learning of others or reduce the time spent on learning. Therefore, it is best to work with students who have motivational problems individually after involving the rest of the class in the day's learning activities. Doing so allows the teacher to protect the class's right to learn and to maximize the time allocated for learning.

II. PREVENTION

Lesson Design

During the 1970s and 1980s, Madeline Hunter (1982), Barak Rosenshine (Rosenshine and Stevens, 1986), and other researchers spent a great deal of time trying to identify the type of lesson structure that was most effective for student learning. Although the various researchers tend to use their own specialized vocabulary, they agree that lessons that include the following components are the most effective in helping students to learn new material: a lesson introduction, clear explanations of the content, checks for student understanding, a period of coached practice, a lesson summary or closure, a period of solitary practice, and periodic reviews. As you read the discussion of these components that follow, remember that a lesson does not equal a class period. A lesson is defined as the amount of instructional time required for students to achieve a specific learning objective. Since a lesson may extend over several class periods, it is not essential to have all of these components in each class period. On the other hand, if one class period contains two lessons, one would expect the components to be repeated twice.

1. *Lesson introduction.* A good introduction makes students aware of what they are supposed to learn, activates their prior knowledge of the topic, focuses their attention on the main elements of the lesson to come, and motivates them to be interested in the lesson.

2. *Clarity.* Clear explanations of the content of the lesson proceed in step-by-step fashion, illustrate the content by using concrete examples familiar to the students, and are interspersed with questions that check student understanding. "Lessons in which learners perceive links among the main ideas are more likely to contribute to content learning than are lessons in which links among the main ideas are less easily perceived by learners" (Anderson, 1989, p. 102). Well-organized presentations help learners to process linking ideas by telling them what prior knowledge should be activated and by pointing out what pieces of information are important in using activated prior knowledge (Anderson, 1989). Techniques for ensuring that presentations are well organized include (a) using structured overviews, advance organizers, and statements of objectives near the beginning of the presentation; (b) outlining the content, signaling transitions between ideas, calling attention to main ideas, and summarizing subsections of the lesson during the presentation; and (c) summarizing main ideas near the end of the presentation.

3. *Coached practice.* Effective lessons include a period of coached or guided practice during which students practice using the skill or knowledge,

7

either through written exercises, oral questions and answers, or some type of group work. This initial practice is closely monitored by the teacher so that students receive frequent feedback and correction. Feedback and correction can occur as frequently as after every two or three problems. Students should experience high amounts of success (over 75 percent) with the coached practice exercises before moving on to solitary practice. Otherwise, they may spend a large portion of the solitary practice period practicing and learning the wrong information or skill.

Wang and Palinscar (1989) cite "scaffolding" as an additional important aspect of the coached practice portion of lessons designed to help students acquire cognitive strategies (such as study skills, problem-solving skills, and critical thinking skills). They cite scaffolding as a process that underlies all of the elements of lesson design. "Scaffolding occurs when the teacher supports students' attempts to use a cognitive strategy; adjusts that support according to learner characteristics, the nature of the material, and the nature of the task; and treats the support as temporary, removing it as students show increased competence in using the cognitive strategy" (p. 79). In other words, the teacher plans instruction to move from modeling and instruction to feedback and coaching, and increasingly transfers control to students.

4. *Closure.* A good lesson summary or closure asks students to become actively involved in summarizing the key ideas that have been learned in the lesson and gives students some ideas about where future lessons will take them.

5. *Solitary practice.* Effective lessons also include a period of solitary or independent practice during which students practice the skill on their own and experience significant amounts of success (over 75 percent). This practice often takes the form of independent seat work or homework. The effectiveness of homework as a tool for promoting learning is directly related to whether it is checked and feedback is provided to students.

6. *Review.* Finally, periodic reviews conducted on a weekly and monthly basis help students to consolidate their learning and provide additional reinforcement.

These six research-based components, which are especially effective in lessons designed to impart basic information or specific skills and procedures, should not be viewed as constraints on the teacher's creativity and individuality. Each component may be embellished and tailored to fit the unique teaching situations that confront every teacher. Together, however, the components provide a basic framework that lessens student confusion about what is to be learned and ensures that learning proceeds in an orderly sequence of steps. When students try to learn more different content before they have mastered prerequisites and when they are not given sufficient practice to master skills, they become confused, disinterested, and much more likely to cause discipline problems in the classroom.

Student Motivation: Teacher Variables

Motivation refers to an inner drive that focuses behavior on a particular goal or task and causes the individual to be persistent in trying to achieve the goal or complete the task successfully. Fostering motivation in students is undoubtedly one of the most powerful tools the teacher has in preventing classroom discipline problems. When students are motivated to learn, they usually pay attention to the lesson, become actively involved in learning, and direct their energies to the task. When students are not motivated to learn, they lose interest in lessons quickly, look for sources of entertainment, and may direct their energies at amusing themselves and disrupting the learning process of others. There are many variables that a professional teacher can manipulate to increase student motivation to learn. According to a review of research on student motivation (Brophy, 1987), some of the most powerful variables are the following:

1. *Student interest.* Teachers can increase student motivation by relating subject content to life outside of school. For example, an English teacher can relate poetry to the lyrics of popular music, and a chemistry teacher can allow students to analyze the chemical composition of products they use. While there is no subject in which every topic can be related to the real world, games, simulations, videos, group work, and allowing students to plan or select activities can increase interest. Although these strategies can't be used effectively every day, they can be employed by all teachers at some time.

2. *Student needs.* Motivation to learn is increased when students perceive that learning activities provide an opportunity to meet some of their basic human needs as identified by Maslow. For example, simply providing elementary students with the opportunity to talk while the whole group listens can be an easy way to help meet students' needs for self-esteem. At the secondary level, allowing students to work together with peers on learning activities helps to meet students' needs for a sense of belonging and acceptance by others. At the most basic level, providing a pleasant, task-oriented climate in which expectations are clear helps to meet students' needs for psychological safety and security.

3. *Novelty and variety.* When the teacher has designed learning activities that include novel events, situations, and materials, students are likely to be motivated to learn. The popcorn lesson in Case 1 is an excellent example of the use of novelty to gain student attention. Once student attention has been captured, a variety of short learning activities will help to keep it focused on the lesson.

Human attention spans can be remarkably long when people are involved in an activity that they find fascinating. Most students, however, do not find typical school activities fascinating. Therefore, their attention spans tend to be rather short. For this reason, the professional teacher plans activities that last no longer than 15 to 20 minutes. A teacher who gives a lecture in two 15-minute halves with a 5-minute oral exercise interspersed is much more likely to maintain student interest than a teacher who gives a 30-minute lecture followed by the 5-minute oral exercise. TV soap operas are an excellent example of how changing the focus of activity every 5 to 10 minutes can hold an audience's attention.

Case 1 • The Popcorn Popper

As Mr. Smith's students walk into tenth-grade creative writing class, they hear an unusual noise. On the teacher's desk an electric popcorn popper filled with unpopped kernels is running. Soon the room is filled with the aroma of fresh popcorn. When the popping is finished, the teacher passes a bowl of popcorn around for everyone to eat. After the students finish eating, Mr. Smith asks them to describe out loud the sights, sounds, smells, taste, and feel of the popcorn. Mr. Smith then uses their accounts as an introduction to a writing exercise on the five senses.

4. *Success.* When students are successful at tasks they perceive to be somewhat challenging, their motivation for future learning is greatly enhanced. It is unreasonable to expect students who fail constantly to have any motivation to participate positively in future learning activities. Thus, it is especially important for teachers to create success for students who are not normally successful. Teachers help to ensure that all students experience some success by making goals and objectives clear, by teaching content clearly in small steps, and by checking to see that students understand each step. Teachers can also encourage success by helping students to acquire the study skills they need when they must work on their own—outlining, note taking, and using textbooks correctly. Still, the most powerful technique for helping students to succeed is to ensure that the material is at the appropriate level of difficulty. Material should be appropriate for the students, given the students' prior learning in that subject.

5. *Tension.* In teaching, tension refers to a feeling of concern or anxiety on the part of the student because she knows that she will be required to demonstrate her learning. A moderate amount of tension increases student learning. When there is no tension in the learning situation, students may be so relaxed that no learning occurs. On the other hand, if there is an overwhelming amount of tension, students may expend more energy in dealing with the tension than they do in learning. Creating a moderate amount of tension results in motivation without tension overload.

When a learning task is inherently interesting and challenging for students, there is little need for the teacher to add tension to the situation. When the learning task is routine and uninteresting for students, a moderate amount of tension created by the teacher enhances motivation and learning. Teacher behaviors that raise the level of tension include moving around the room, calling on volunteers and nonvolunteers to answer questions in a random pattern, giving quizzes on class material, checking homework and seat work, and reminding students that they will be tested on the material they are learning.

6. *Feeling tone.* Feeling tone refers to the emotional atmosphere or climate in the classroom. According to Madeline Hunter (1982), classroom feeling tone can be extremely positive, moderately positive, neutral, moderately negative, and extremely negative. An extremely positive feeling tone can be so sweet that it actually directs student attention away from learning, a neutral feeling tone is bland and nonstimulating, and an extremely negative feeling tone is threatening and may produce a tension overload. The most effective feeling tone is a moderately positive one in which the atmosphere is pleasant and friendly but clearly focused on the learning task at hand. The teacher can help to create such a feeling tone by making a room that is comfortable and pleasantly decorated, by treating students in a courteous and friendly manner, by expressing sincere interest in students as individuals, and by communicating positively with students both verbally and nonverbally. See how one teacher expresses his interest in students in Case 2.

Although a moderately positive feeling tone is the most motivating one, it is sometimes necessary to create, temporarily, a moderately negative feeling tone. If students are not doing their work and not living up to their responsibilities, it is necessary to shake them out of their complacency with some well-chosen, corrective comments. The wise teacher understands that undesirable consequences may result from a classroom feeling tone that is continuously negative and, therefore, works to create a moderately positive classroom climate most of the time.

Case 2 • Talking between Classes

Mr. Dailey, the eighth-grade English teacher, does not spend the time in between classes standing out in the hallway or visiting with friends. Instead he uses the three minutes to chat with individual students. During these chats, he talks with students about their out-of-school activities, their hobbies, their feelings about school and his class in particular, their plans and aspirations, and everyday school events. He feels that these three-minute chats really promote a more positive feeling tone in his classroom and allow him to relate to his students as individuals.

7. *Feedback.* Because it provides both information that can be used to improve performance and a yardstick or criterion by which progress can be measured, feedback also increases motivation. Feedback is most effective when it is specific and is delivered soon after or at the time of performance. Teachers usually provide feedback in the form of oral and written comments on tests and assignments. One additional way to use feedback as a motivator is to have students keep track of their own progress over time and to provide periodic opportunities for them to reflect on their progress.

8. *Encouragement.* Encouragement is a great motivator. It emphasizes the positive aspects of behavior; recognizes and validates real effort; communicates positive expectations for future behavior; and communicates that the teacher trusts, respects, and believes in the child. All too frequently, teachers and parents point out how children have failed to meet expectations. Pointing out shortcomings and focusing on past transgressions erode children's self-esteem, whereas encouraging communication, as defined by Sweeney (1981), enhances self-esteem. It emphasizes present and future behavior rather than past transgressions and what is being learned and done correctly rather than on what has not been learned.

Ms. Johnson in Case 3 would have had a far more positive impact on Heidi's motivation if she had pointed out the positive aspects of Heidi's work as well as the error in spelling. After all, a child who gets a 68 on an exam has learned twice as much as she has failed to learn. For more on encouragement, see Dreikurs's Children the Challenge (1964).

Case 3 • Nonconstructive Feedback

Ms. Johnson was handing back the seventh-graders' reports on their library books. Heidi waited anxiously to get her report back. She had read a book on archaeology and had really gotten into it. She spent quite a bit of time explaining in her report how neat it must be to be able to relive the past by examining the artifacts people left behind. When she received her book report, Heidi was dejected. The word artifact—Heidi had spelled it artafact—was circled twice on her paper with sp written above it. At the bottom of the paper, Ms. Johnson had written, "spelling errors are careless and are not acceptable." The only other mark Ms. Johnson had made on the paper was a grade of C.

12

How can you use these research findings to improve student motivation in your own classroom? Ask yourself the following questions as you plan classroom activities for your students:

1. How can I make use of natural student interests in this learning activity?
2. How can I help students to meet their basic human needs in this activity?
3. How can I use novel events and/or materials in this activity?
4. How can I provide for variety in these learning activities?
5. How can I ensure that my students will be successful?
6. How can I create an appropriate level of tension for this learning task?
7. How can I create a moderately pleasant feeling tone for this activity?
8. How can I provide feedback to students and help them to recognize their progress in learning?
9. How can I encourage my students?

This list of nine questions is also an important resource when discipline problems occur. By answering the questions, the teacher may find ways to increase the motivation to learn and decrease the motivation to misbehave.

Teacher Expectations

Teacher expectations influence both student learning and student motivation. Beginning in the 1970s, researchers such as Thomas Good and Jere Brophy conducted observational studies of teacher behavior toward students whom the teachers perceived as high achievers and students they perceived as low achievers. Multiple research studies found that teachers often unintentionally communicate low expectations toward students whom they perceive as low achievers. These lower expectations are communicated by behaviors such as:

1. Calling on low achievers less often to answer questions.
2. Giving low achievers less think time when they are called on.
3. Providing fewer clues and hints to low achievers when they have initial difficulty in answering questions.
4. Praising correct answers from low achievers less often.
5. Criticizing wrong answers from low achievers more often.
6. Praising marginal answers from low achievers but demanding more precise answers from high achievers.

13

7. Staying farther away physically and psychologically from low achievers.
8. Rarely expressing personal interest in low achievers.
9. Smiling less frequently at low achievers.
10. Making eye contact less frequently with low achievers.
11. Complimenting low achievers less often.

Some of these behaviors may be motivated by good intentions on the part of the teacher, who, for example, may give low achievers less think time to avoid embarrassing them if they don't know an answer. However, the cumulative effect is the communication of a powerful message: "I don't expect you to be able to do much." This message triggers a vicious cycle. Students begin to expect less of themselves, produce less, and confirm the teacher's original perception of them. While in many cases the teacher may have a legitimate reason to expect less from some students, communicating low expectations produces only negative effects.

Researchers have demonstrated that when teachers equalize response opportunities, feedback, and personal involvement, student learning can improve. The message is clear. Communicating high expectations to all learners appears to influence low achievers to learn more, whereas communicating low expectations, no matter how justified, has a debilitating effect (Good and Brophy, 1987).

Although empirical research in this area has been limited to the effects of teacher expectations on achievement, we believe that the generalizations hold true for student behavior as well. Communicating high expectations for student behavior is likely to bring about increased positive behaviors; communicating low expectations for student behavior is likely to bring about increased negative behavior. A teacher who says, "I am sure that all of you will complete all of your homework assignments carefully because you realize that doing homework is an important way of practicing what you are learning" is more likely to have students complete homework assignments than a teacher who says, "I know you probably don't like to do homework, but if you fail to complete homework assignments, it will definitely lower your grades." As Brophy (1988a) has noted: "Consistent projection of positive expectations, attributions and social labels to the students is important in fostering positive self-concepts and related motives that orient them toward prosocial behavior. In short, students who are consistently treated as if they are well-intentioned individuals who respect themselves and others and desire to act responsibly, morally, and prosocially are more likely to live up to those expectations and acquire those qualities than students who are treated as if they had the opposite qualities" (p. 11). Given the powerful research results in this area, all teachers should step back and reflect on the expectations they communicate to students through their verbal and nonverbal classroom behavior.

Student Motivation: Student Cognition

In this section we will look at motivation from the perspective of student cognition and its impact on motivation to learn. There are at present at least three theories of student motivation—student cognition, attribution, and expectancy x value theory—that have interesting implications for teaching.

The primary developer of the social cognition theory of student motivation was A. Bandura (1986). Bandura took issue with the behavioral notions of motivation that emphasized external reinforcers. He asserted that the individual's thoughts play a central role not only in determining the individual's motivational levels but also in determining how the individual will perceive variables that are intended to be reinforcers. Bandura's research demonstrated that personal evaluation and self-satisfaction are potent reinforcers of behavior, in fact probably more potent than reinforcers provided by others. Bandura's research findings showed that involving students in personal goal setting and providing frequent opportunities for them to monitor and reflect on their progress toward these goals can increase student learning efforts. In fact, according to Bandura, external praise can diminish self-evaluation and create dependency on others, thereby reducing an individual's intrinsic motivation to succeed.

Bandura's work on personal evaluation and self-satisfaction led to a related concept that he called self-efficacy. Self-efficacy refers to an individual's expectation of success at a particular task. When feelings of self-efficacy are high, individuals are much more likely to exert effort toward task completion than they are when feelings are low because they believe they have the potential to be successful. When feelings of self-efficacy are low, efforts are diminished. Feelings of self-efficacy develop from judgments about past performance as well as from vicarious observations of others in similar situations. The greater the perceived similarity between the person we are observing (the model) and ourselves, the greater the impact their fate will have on our own feelings of self-efficacy.

When the social cognition theory is in action in the classroom, the task of the teacher is to focus encouragement on the improvement of individual effort and achievement over time. Teachers who wish to use this theory in the classroom should begin by engaging students in setting personal goals that are concrete, specific, and realistic. Teachers then involve students in monitoring their own performance toward the achievement of these goals. When students are successful, teachers encourage them to engage in self-reinforcement so that

15

they will build positive feelings of self-efficacy toward the accomplishment of future tasks.

Attribution theory deals with student perceived causes of success and failure in school tasks. Clearly, student perceptions of why they succeed or fail at school tasks have a direct impact on their motivation to perform (Stipek, 1993). Research has identified five factors to which students are likely to attribute success or failure. These factors are ability, effort, task difficulty, luck, and other people such as the teacher (Ames and Ames, 1984). The only factor that can be controlled directly by the student is effort. When students attribute success to effort and failure to lack of effort or inappropriate types of effort, they are likely to exert additional effort in the future. "Students who believe that their personal efforts influence their learning are more likely to learn than those who believe that learning depends on teachers or other factors such as task difficulty or luck" (Wang and Palinscar, 1989).

When students attribute failure to lack of ability, the impact on future performance is devastating. Negative feelings of self-efficacy develop, and students see little value in making any effort since they believe that they are not likely to be successful. As negative judgments of ability become more internalized and self-worth more damaged, students stop making any effort as a defense mechanism. Not making the effort allows them to protect their self-concept from further damage. They can simply shrug their shoulders and claim, "I could have done it if I wanted to, but I really didn't think it was worth it." This face-saving device prevents the further ego damage that would result from additional negative ability attributions. To avoid setting up the vicious cycle of failure and lack of future effort, teachers need to recognize the danger of placing students in competitive situations in which they do not have the ability to compete, or of asking students to complete tasks that are too difficult for them.

The implications of attribution theory for classroom teaching are clear. Students need to be assigned tasks that are moderately challenging but within their capability. This may mean that the teacher has to break complex tasks into subtasks that the student can handle and provide a great deal of scaffolding for the student, especially early in the learning process. The teacher should encourage students to make the right kind of effort in completing classroom tasks. When students are successful, the teacher can attribute their success to this effort. When students are not successful, the teacher may want to focus attention on the lack of effort or on using inappropriate strategies. Research has demonstrated that teacher statements concerning attributions for success or failure are the key variable in influencing students to attribute success or failure to one variable rather than another.

The expectancy x value theory proposes that the effort that an individual is willing to put forth in any task is directly related to the product of two factors: the belief that he will be successful and the value of the outcomes

16

that will be gained through successful completion of the task (Feathers, 1982). A multiplication sign is used to indicate the interaction between the two factors. Note that if either of the two factors is 0, no effort will be put forth. Thus, if a students believes that he has the potential to be successful in academic work and values good grades and the other outcomes that accompany academic success, he will be highly motivated to put forth a strong effort. On the other hand, if the student doubts his ability to perform the academic tasks successfully or does not value good grades and the other outcomes attached to academic success, he is likely to put forth a limited effort. Teachers can increase a student's effort at success either by encouraging the learner to believe that he can be successful or by increasing the value of the outcomes.

Good and Brophy (1997) have suggested that teachers should take the following steps to take advantage of the expectancy x value theory in the classroom: (1) establish a supportive classroom climate, (2) structure activities so that they are at the appropriate level of difficulty, (3) develop learning objectives that have personal meaning and relevance for the students, and (4) engage students in personal goal setting and self-appraisal. Finally, for the expectancy x value theory to succeed, the teacher needs to help students recognize the link between effort and outcome suggested by attribution theory.

Classroom Procedures

There are two types of classroom guidelines, procedures and rules. Procedures are routines that call for specified behaviors at particular times or during particular activities. Procedures are directed at accomplishing something, not at managing disruptive behavior. Examples of procedures include standard ways of passing out and turning in materials, entering and leaving the room, and taking attendance. Procedures reflect behaviors necessary for the smooth operation of the classroom and soon become an integral part of the running of the classroom.

Procedures are taught to students through examples and demonstrations. Properly designed and learned, procedures maximize on-task student behavior by minimizing the need for students to ask for directions and the need for teachers to give instructions for everyday classroom events. Certain important procedures, for example, steps to be followed during fire drills and appropriate heading information for tests and assignments, may be prominently displayed for students' reference.

Because students often do not learn and use a teacher's procedures immediately, feedback and practice must be provided. However the time spent on teaching the procedures is well invested and eventually leads to a successful management system (Brophy, 1988b). Often in art, science, and elementary classes, which are quite procedurally oriented, teachers have students practice the required procedures. In classrooms in which procedures are directly related

17

to safety or skill development (such as equipment handling in industrial arts or science laboratory techniques), instructional objectives involving the procedures are used in addition to subject matter objectives. In these situations, the procedures become an integral part of the classroom instruction.

The use of natural and logical consequences is quite appropriate for students who fail to follow procedural guidelines. Natural consequences are outcomes of behavior that occur without teacher intervention. Examples of natural consequences are the inability of a teacher to record a student's grade if an assignment is handed in without a name and the incorrect results that occur because of inappropriate laboratory procedures (if not a safety hazard).

The use of logical consequences is much more common and has wider applicability in school settings than the use of natural ones. Logical consequences are outcomes that are directly related to the behavior but require teacher intervention to occur. Examples of logical consequences are students having less time for recess because they did not line up correctly to leave the room and students having to pay for the damage to their textbooks because of careless use.

Natural and logical consequences are powerful management concepts because the consequences that students experience are directly related to their behavior. In addition, because it is only the student who is responsible for the consequences, the teacher is removed from the role of punisher.

Classroom Rules

In contrast to procedures, rules focus on appropriate behavior. They provide the guidelines for those behaviors that are required if teaching and learning are to take place. Because they cover a wider spectrum of behavior than procedures, the development of rules is usually a more complex and time-consuming task.

The Need for Rules. Schools in general and classrooms in particular are dynamic places. Within almost any given classroom, learning activities vary widely and may range from individual seat work to large group projects that necessitate cooperative working arrangements among students. While this dynamism helps to motivate student learning, human behavior is highly sensitive to differing conditions across situations as well as to changing conditions within situations (Walker, 1979). Evidence indicates that children in general and disruptive children in particular are highly sensitive to changing situations and conditions (Johnson, Boadstad, and Lobitz, 1976; Kazdin and Bootzin, 1972). Given this, the need for rules is apparent.

Rules should be directed at organizing the learning environment to ensure the continuity and quality of teaching and learning and not at exerting control over students (Brophy, 1988a). Appropriately designed rules increase on-task student behavior and result in improved learning.

Determining Necessary Rules. A long list of do's and don'ts is one sure way to reduce the likelihood that rules will be effective. Teachers who attempt to cover every conceivable classroom behavior with a rule place themselves in the untenable position of having to observe and monitor the most minute and insignificant student behaviors. This leaves little time for teaching. Students, especially in upper elementary and secondary grades, view a long list of do's and don'ts as picky and impossible to follow. They regard teachers who monitor and correct every behavior as nagging, unreasonable, and controlling.

Teachers must develop individually or with students a list of rules that is fair, realistic, and can be rationalized as necessary for the development of an appropriate classroom environment (Emmer et al., 1997). To do this, the teacher, before meeting a class for the first time, must seriously consider the question "What are the necessary student behaviors that I need in my classroom so that discipline problems will not occur?" To assist in answering this question, keep in mind this definition of a discipline problem: *A discipline problem is any behavior that interferes with the teaching act, interferes with the rights of others to learn, is psychologically or physically unsafe, or destroys property.* Thus, any rule that is developed by the teacher or by the teacher and students jointly must be able to be rationalized as necessary to ensure that (1) the teacher's right to teach is protected, (2) the students' rights to learning are protected, (3) the students' psychological and physical safety are protected, and (4) property is protected. Rules that are so developed and rationalized make sense to students because they are not arbitrary. Such rules also lend themselves to the use of natural and logical consequences when students do not follow them.

Developing Consequences. When students choose not to follow classroom rules, they should experience consequences (Canter, 1989). The type of consequences and how they are applied may determine whether or not students follow rules and whether or not they respect the teacher. Therefore, the development of appropriate consequences is as important as the development of the rules themselves.

Unfortunately teachers usually give considerably more thought to the design of rules than they do to the design of consequences. When a rule is not followed, teachers often simply determine the consequence on the spot. Such an approach may lead to inconsistent, irrational consequences that are interpreted by students as unfair, unreasonable, and unrelated to their behavior. This view of the teacher's behavior eventually undermines the teacher's effectiveness as a classroom manager and leads to more disruptive student behavior.

Although consequences should be planned in advance by the teacher, there is some debate about whether or not students should know in advance what the consequences will be. Some teachers feel that sharing potential consequences helps students to live up to teacher expectations and avoids later complaints about the fairness of the consequences. Other teachers believe that announcing consequences in advance gives students the impression that the teacher expects students not to live up to expectations. They prefer to act as if they have no need to think about consequences since they know that all the students will be successful in meeting both behavioral and academic expectations. There is no empirical answer to this debate. It is a matter of teacher beliefs and preference.

Communicating Rules. If the teacher decides to develop classroom rules by herself, she must communicate the rules clearly to the students (Canter, 1992; Evertson and Emmer, 1982; Jones and Jones, 1998). Clear communication entails a discussion of what the rules are and a rationale for each and every one (Good and Brophy, 1997). When students understand the purpose of rules, they are likely to view them as reasonable and fair, which increases the likelihood of appropriate behavior.

The manner in which rules are phrased is important. Certain rules need to be stated so that it is clear that they apply to both the teacher and the students. This is accomplished by using the phrase, "We all need to" followed by the behavioral expectation and the rationale. For example, the teacher might say, "We all need to pay attention and not interrupt when someone is speaking because it is important to respect each other's right to participate and voice his views." Such phrasing incorporates the principle that teachers must model the behaviors they expect (Brophy, 1988a).

Although it is essential for the teacher to communicate behavioral expectations and the rationales behind them, in many cases this does not ensure student understanding and acceptance of the rules. A final critical strategy, then, is to obtain from each student a strong indication that he understands the rules as well as a commitment to attempting to abide by them (Jones and Jones, 1998).

Obtaining Commitments. When two or more people reach an agreement, they often finalize it with a handshake or a signed contract to indicate that the individuals intend to comply with the terms of the agreement. While agreements are often violated, a handshake, verbal promise, or written contract increases the probability that the agreement will be kept. With this idea in mind, it is a wise teacher who has his students express their understanding of the rules and their intent to abide by them.

20

The Cultural Embeddedness of Rules and Guidelines

When teachers are establishing and teaching classroom rules and procedures, they need to remember that their students come from a variety of cultural backgrounds. Culture refers to the knowledge, customs, rituals, emotions, traditions, values, and norms shared by members of a population and embodied in a set of behaviors designed for survival in a particular environment. Because students come to the classroom from different cultural backgrounds, they bring with them different values, norms, and behavioral expectations. Traditionally, teachers have acted as if everyone shared the same cultural expectations and have ignored cultural differences. However, this does not appear to be a wise strategy. Schools and classrooms are not culturally neutral or culture free. Most schools follow the values, norms, and behavioral patterns of middle-class, white, European cultures. As Irvine (1990) has pointed out, however, these values and norms differ in significant ways from the values, norms, and behavioral expectations found in nondominant cultural groups such as African Americans, Hispanic Americans, and Native Americans.

Because of cultural differences, many children from underrepresented groups experience cultural dissonance or lack of cultural synchronization in school; that is, teachers and students are out of step with each other when it comes to their expectations for appropriate behavior. Cultural synchronization is an extremely important factor in the establishment of positive relationships between teachers and students. According to Jeanette Abi-Nader (1993), one of the most solidly substantiated principles in communication theory is the principle of homophily, which holds that the more two people are alike in background, attitudes, perceptions, and values the more effectively they will communicate with each other and the more similar they will become. A lack of cultural synchronization leads to misunderstandings between teachers and students that can and often do result in conflict, distrust, hostility, and possibly school failure (Irvine, 1990). "The typical experience in the school is a denigration of African and African American culture. Indeed there is a denial of its very existence. The language that students bring with them to school is seen to be deficient—a corruption of English. The familial organization is considered pathological. And the historical, cultural, and scientific contributions of African Americans are ignored or trivialized" (Ladson-Billings, 1994, p. 138).

To illustrate his discussion of the importance of cultural synchronization, Irvine has pointed out several differences in cultural style between whites and African Americans. We will use these differences in the following discussion simply as an illustration of the influence of culture on values, norms, and expectations. We recognize, as does Irvine, that these attributes are neither representative of all African Americans nor all white Americans. It would, of course, be possible to use any other nondominant

21

cultural group to illustrate such differences. With these caveats in mind, we now turn to some of the differences in style identified by Irvine.

African Americans tend to be more high key, more animated, more intense, and more confrontational than whites. African Americans tend to appreciate social contexts in which overlapping speech and participatory dialogue are used rather than turn taking in which only one person is free to speak at any given time. African Americans tend to favor passionate, emotional argumentation in defense of beliefs as opposed to the nonemotional, uninvolved, logical argumentation preferred by whites. African Americans tend to have a relational, field-dependent learning style as opposed to the analytical, field-independent style of learning characteristic of most whites. While whites prefer confined or restricted movement, African Americans tend to learn better through freedom of movement. Finally, African Americans tend to have a much greater people focus than whites during learning activities and tend to favor modes of learning in which they are interactive with others. As a result of these differences in cultural style, African Americans often find their expressive behavior style criticized in contexts in which white standards of behavior prevail (Kochman, 1981).

Differences in values, norms, and expectations resulting from cultural differences have several implications for teachers. First, teachers must understand that schools are culturally situated institutions. The values, norms, and behaviors promoted by schools are never culturally neutral. They are always influenced by some particular cultural mindset. Therefore, school and classroom rules and guidelines must be seen as culturally derived. Second, teachers should strive to learn more about the cultural backgrounds of the students they teach. This can be accomplished by observing how students believe in other contexts, by talking to students about their behavior and allowing them to teach about their behavior, by involving parents and community members in the classroom, and by participating in community events and learning more about the institutions in the students' home community. "Students are less likely to fail in school settings where they feel positive about both their own culture and the majority culture and are not alienated from their own cultural values" (Cummins [1986] in Ladson-Billings, 1994, p. 11). Third, teachers should acknowledge and intentionally incorporate students' cultural backgrounds and expectations into their classrooms. When teacher rules and expectations are in conflict with student cultural expectations, it may be appropriate to reexamine and renegotiate rules and procedures. At the very least, students need to be provided with a clear rationale for why the rules and procedures are important. It goes without saying that the rationale for the rules should be in keeping with the four guidelines articulated earlier in the chapter. Finally, when students behave inappropriately, teachers should step back and examine the behavior in terms of the student's cultural background. Using a different set of cultural lenses to view behavior may shed a very different light on the teacher's perceptions of individual students. Obviously, misbehavior that results from differences in cultural background and expectations should be handled quite differently from misbehavior that signifies intentional disruption on the part of the student.

Creating Group Norms to Structure Appropriate Behavior

Although students and teachers bring their own cultural backgrounds with them, each classroom tends to develop its own culture, that is, certain norms develop over time that exert a great influence on student behavior.

Traditionally, teachers have ignored the notion of peer culture and group norms in the classroom. They have focused their attention on individual learners and have viewed influencing students to behave appropriately as an issue between the teacher and the individual student. As a result, the development of group norms among students has been left almost completely up to chance. However, there is growing evidence that teachers can intervene to create group norms that will promote prosocial behavior as well as lead to peer relationships that will enhance the four components of self-esteem identified earlier: significance, power, competence, and virtue. Cooperative learning lessons that include face-to-face interaction, positive interdependence, and individual accountability can help to establish positive group norms. When teachers make a concentrated effort to help students develop the social skills necessary to function effectively as group members during cooperative learning activities, they enhance the power of cooperative learning activities to create positive group norms.

Johnson, Johnson, and Holubec (1993) have identified four sets of skills—forming skills, functioning skills, formulating skills, and fermenting skills—that students need to develop over time in order to function most effectively as a group. When these skills are in place and groups function successfully, group norms develop that lead students to (1) be engaged in learning activities, (2) strive toward learning and achievement, and (3) interact with each other in ways that will facilitate the development of positive self-esteem.

Forming skills are an initial set of management skills that are helpful in getting groups up and running smoothly and effectively. These skills include moving into groups quietly without bothering others, staying with the group rather than moving around the room, using quiet voices that can be heard by members of the group but not by others, and encouraging all group members to participate.

Functioning skills are group-management skills aimed at controlling the types of interactions that occur among group members. These skills include staying focused on the task, expressing support and acceptance of others, asking for help or clarification, offering to explain or clarify, and paraphrasing or summarizing what others have said.

Formulating skills refer to a set of behaviors that help students to process material mentally. These skills include summarizing key points, connecting ideas to each other, seeking elaboration of ideas, finding ways to remember information more effectively, and checking explanations and ideas through articulation.

Finally, fermenting skills are a set of skills needed to resolve cognitive conflicts that arise within the group. These skills include criticizing ideas without criticizing people, synthesizing diverse ideas, asking for justification, extending other people's ideas, and probing for more information.

Johnson, Johnson, and Holubec (1993) suggest that teachers teach these social skills just as they teach academic content. Therefore, when teachers plan a cooperative learning activity, they must plan social skill objectives as well as the academic objectives. Making the social skills explicit as lesson objectives helps to focus both student and teacher attention on them. To do this the teacher should explain the skill before the activity begins and make sure students know what the skill looks like and sounds like as it is expressed in behavior. Once the teacher is convinced that students understand the meaning of the skill, students may practice the skill during the cooperative learning activity. While the students are practicing, the teacher moves from group to group monitoring the use of the skill. When the activity has been completed, the teacher engages each group in reflecting on how successfully the skill was used and in setting goals for improving their use of the skill in the future. Although teaching social skills in addition to academic content takes time, the time is well spent for two reasons. First, many of these skills are exactly the kinds of skills students will need to help them succeed as adults. Second, when students are skilled at interacting with each other in positive ways, group norms develop in the classroom that are supportive of prosocial behavior and of engagement in appropriate learning activities.

III. MANAGING COMMON MISBEHAVIOR PROBLEMS

Proactive Intervention Skills

Developing expertise in the use of the following proactive skills should lessen the need for more intrusive management techniques.

1. *Changing the pace of classroom activities.* Rubbing eyes, yawning, stretching, and staring out the window are clear signs that a change of pace is needed. This is the time for the teacher to restructure the situation and involve students in games, stories, or other favorite activities that require active student participation and help to refocus student interests. To reduce the need for on-the-spot change-of-pace activities, lesson plans should provide for a variety of learning experiences that accommodate the attention spans and interests of the students both in time and in type.

2. *Removing seductive objects.* The skill may be used with little, if any, pause in the teaching act. However, there should be an agreement that the objects will be returned after class. Teachers who find themselves competing with toys, magazines, or combs may simply walk over to the student, collect the object, and quietly inform the student that it will be available after class.

3. *Interest boosting of a student who shows signs of off-task behavior.* Rather than using other, less-positive techniques, the teacher shows interest in the student's work, thereby bringing the student back on-task. Interest boosting is often called for when students are required to do individual or small group classwork. It is during these times that the potential for chatter, daydreaming, or other off-task behaviors is high. If the teacher observes a student engaging in activities other than the assigned math problems, for example, she can boost the interest of the student by walking over to the student and asking how the work is going or checking the answers of the completed problems. Asking the student to place correct problems on the board is also effective. Whatever technique is decided on, it must be employed in a matter-of-fact supportive manner to boost the student's interest in the learning activity.

4. *Redirecting the behavior of off-task students.* This skill helps to refocus the student's attention. Students who are passing notes, talking, or daydreaming may be asked to read, do a problem, or answer a question. When this technique is used, it is important to treat the student as if she were paying attention. For instance, if you call on the off-task student to answer a question and the student answers correctly, give positive feedback. If she doesn't answer or answers incorrectly, reformulate the question or call on someone else. A teacher who causes the student embarrassment or ridicule by stating, "You would know where we were if you were paying attention" invites further misbehavior. The "get back on-task" message the teacher is sending is clearly received by the off-task student whether or not she answers the question or finds the proper reading place and does not require any negative comments.

5. *Nonpunitive time out.* This skill should be used for students who show signs of encountering a provoking, painful, frustrating, or fatiguing situation. The teacher quietly asks the student if she would like to get a drink or invites her to run an errand or do a chore. The change in activity gives the student time to regain her control before reentering the learning environment. Teachers must be alert to the signs of frustration so they can act in a timely fashion to help students cope.

6. *Encouraging the appropriate behavior of other students.* A statement such as "I'm glad to see that Joan and Andrea have their books open" reminds off-task students of the behavior that is expected of them.

7. *Providing cues for expected behaviors.* Cues can be quite effective in obtaining the desired behavior, but the teacher must be sure the cue is understood by all. For example, a teacher who expects students to be in their seats and prepared for class when the bell rings, must make sure that everyone understands that the bell signals the start of class. In schools without bells or other indicators, closing the door is an appropriate cue. Some teachers flick the lights to cue a class that the noise has reached unacceptable levels. Using the same cues consistently usually results in quick student response.

Remedial Intervention Skills

The masterful use of proactive skills diffuses many surface behaviors and causes minimal disruptions to the teaching act. However, there will always be classroom situations that induce misbehavior or students who continue to display disruptive behaviors.

These behaviors may range from mildly off-task to very disruptive. Mastering the delivery of intervention skills should help to produce an exceptional classroom in which misbehavior is minimized and teachers are free to teach and children are free to learn.

Before any intervention may be used, the teacher must have a basis on which to make decisions concerning common inappropriate behaviors in the classroom. To avoid inconsistency and arbitrariness, teachers must also have a systematic intervention plan of predetermined behaviors that clearly communicates disapproval to the student who calls out, throws paper, walks around, passes notes, or in any way interferes with the teaching or learning act (Canter, 1989; Lasley, 1989).

26

The intervention decision-making approach is a sequence of hierarchically ordered teacher behaviors. Because we believe that students must learn to control their own behavior, the initial interventions are subtle, nonintrusive, and very student centered. Although these behaviors communicate disapproval, they are designed to provide students with the opportunity to control their own behavior. If the misbehaviors are not curbed, the interventions become increasingly more intrusive and teacher centered; that is, the teacher takes more responsibility for managing the students' behavior.

Because we also believe that management techniques should not in themselves disrupt the teaching and learning act (Brophy, 1988), early intervention behaviors are almost a private communication between the teacher and the off-task student. They alert the student to her inappropriate behavior but cause little if any noticeable disruption to either teaching or learning. If these nonverbal interventions, which make up the first tier of the decision-making hierarchy, are not successful, they are followed by the second and third tiers: teacher verbal behaviors and consequences. These tiers are increasingly more teacher centered, more intrusive, and may cause some interruption to the teaching/learning act.

The decision-making hierarchy described is intended to be a dynamic model, not one that binds a teacher into a lockstep, sequential, cookbook intervention approach. Instead the model requires the teacher to make a decision as to which intervention in the hierarchy to employ first. The decision should depend on the type and frequency of the disruptive behavior and should be congruent with five implementation guidelines that follow. These guidelines should help to ensure that any beginning intervention, as well as those that may follow, meets the two foundational precepts of the hierarchy: increasing student self-control and decreasing disruptions to the teaching and learning environment.

1. The intervention provides a student with opportunities for the self-control of the disruptive behaviors. Self-control is not developed to its fullest in classrooms where teachers immediately intervene with teacher-centered techniques to manage student behavior. Because we believe individuals make conscious choices to behave in certain ways and that individuals cannot be forced to learn or exhibit appropriate behavior, early interventions should not force students but rather influence them to manage themselves. Students must be given responsibility in order to learn responsibility.

2. The intervention does not cause more disruption to the teaching and learning environment than the disruptive behavior itself. We have all witnessed teacher interventions that were more disruptive to the class than the off-task student behavior. This usually occurs when the teacher uses an intervention too far up the decision-making hierarchy. For example, the teacher chooses to use a

27

public verbal technique when a private nonverbal intervention would be more effective and less disruptive. When this happens the teacher becomes more of a disruptive factor than the student.

3. The intervention lessens the probability that the student will become more disruptive or confrontational. Interventions should lessen and defuse confrontational situations. When teachers choose to employ public, aggressive, or humiliating techniques, they increase the likelihood of escalating confrontations and power struggles. Again, deciding where in the decision-making hierarchy to begin has a significant effect on whether a disruptive student will be brought back on task or will become confrontational.

4. The intervention protects students from physical and psychological harm and does not cause physical or psychological harm. When a teacher observes behaviors that could be harmful to any student, intervention should be swift and teacher- centered. In such situations, nonverbal techniques are usually bypassed for the assertive delivery of verbal interventions. In all cases we must be careful that the interventions are not in themselves a source of harm to students or to the teacher.

5. The choice of the specific intervention maximizes the number of alternatives left for the teacher to use if it becomes necessary. Every teacher knows that it often takes more than one intervention to manage student behavior. It is rare that disruptive behavior is noted, a teacher intervention occurs, and the student is back on task forever. It is the unwise teacher who sends a student out of the classroom for the first occurrence of a disruptive behavior. Such an intervention leaves few options available to the teacher if the student continues to misbehave when she returns. By using the decision-making hierarchy of intervention skills, the teacher reserves many alternative interventions.

It is important to remember that the teacher's goal in employing any remedial intervention skill is to redirect the student to appropriate behavior. Stopping the misbehavior may be the initial step in the process, but it is not sufficient. The teacher's goal is not reached until the student becomes reengaged in learning activities. Thus, whenever the teacher is introduced to a new technique for dealing with disruptive behavior, one of the questions she should ask in determining whether to employ the technique is, "Is this technique likely to redirect the student to appropriate behavior?"

The first tier of the hierarchy of remedial intervention skills, nonverbal skills, consists of four techniques: planned ignoring, signal interference, proximity interference, and touch interferencer. These body-language interventions were first identified by Redl and Wineman (1952). When they are used randomly, effective management of minor disruptions is not fully achieved. However, when they are consciously employed in a predetermined logical sequence, they serve to curb milder forms of off-task behavior (Shrigley, 1985).

Planned Ignoring

Planned ignoring is based on the reinforcement theory that if you ignore a behavior, it will lessen and eventually disappear. Although this sounds simple, it is difficult to ignore a behavior completely. That is why *planned* is stressed. When a student whistles, interrupts the teacher, or calls out, the teacher instinctively looks in the direction of the student, thereby giving the student attention and reinforcing the behavior. In contrast, planned ignoring intentionally and completely ignores the behavior. This takes practice.

There are limitations to this intervention. First, according to reinforcement theory, when a behavior has been reinforced previously, removal of the reinforcement causes a short-term increase in the behavior in the hope of again receiving reinforcement. Thus, when planned ignoring is first used, there probably will be an increase of the off-task behavior. Therefore, this technique should be used to manage only the behaviors that cause little interference to the teaching/learning act (Brophy, 1988). Second, the disruptive behavior often is being reinforced by the other students who attend to the misbehaving student. If it is, planned ignoring by the teacher has little effect.

The behaviors that usually are managed by planned ignoring are not having materials ready for the start of class, calling out answers rather than raising a hand, mild or infrequent whispering, interrupting the teacher, and daydreaming. Obviously the type of learning activity has much to do with the behaviors that can or cannot be ignored. If, after a reasonable period of time of ignoring the off-task behavior, the behavior does not decrease or the point is reached at which others are distracted by it, the teacher has to move quickly and confidently to the next step in the hierarchy, signal interference.

Signal Interference

Signal interference is any type of nonverbal behavior that communicates to the student without disturbing others that the behavior is not appropriate. Signal interventions must be clearly directed at the off-task student. There should be no doubt in the student's mind that the teacher is aware of what is going on and that the student is responsible for the behavior. The teacher's expression should be businesslike. It is ineffective for the teacher to make eye contact with a student and smile. Smiling sends a double message, which confuses students and may be interpreted as a lack of seriousness by the teacher.

Examples of signal interference behaviors are making eye contact with the student who is talking to a neighbor, pointing to a seat when a student is wandering around, head shaking to indicate "no" to a student who is about to throw a paper airplane, and holding up an open hand to stop a student's calling out. Like all coping skills, signal interference behaviors may be hierarchically

29

ordered, depending on the type, duration, and frequency of off-task behavior. A simple hand motion may serve to manage calling out the first time, whereas direct eye contact with a disapproving look may be needed the next time the student calls out.

For disruptive behaviors that continue or for disturbances that more seriously affect others' learning, the teacher moves to the next intervention skill in the hierarchy, proximity interference.

Proximity Interference

Proximity interference is any movement toward the disruptive student. When signal interference doesn't work, or the teacher is unable to gain a student's attention long enough to send a signal because the student is so engrossed in the off-task behavior, proximity interference is warranted.

Often just walking toward the student while conducting the lesson is enough to bring the student back on task. If the student continues to be off task, the teacher may want to conduct the lesson in close proximity to the student's desk, which is usually quite effective. This technique works well during question-and-answer periods.

Proximity interference combined with signal interference results in a very effective nonverbal management technique. It's the rare student who is not brought back on task by a teacher who makes eye contact and begins walking toward her desk. Like signal interference, proximity interference techniques may be hierarchically ordered from nonchalant movement in the direction of the student to an obvious standing behind or next to the student during class. If proximity does not bring about the desired behavioral change, the teacher is in a position to implement the next step in the coping skill hierarchy, touch interference.

Touch Interference

When a teacher takes a child's hand and escorts the child back to her seat or when a teacher places a hand on a student's shoulder, she is using touch interference. Touch interference is a light, nonaggressive physical contact with the student. Without any verbal exchange, touch interference communicates to the student that the teacher disapproves of the disruptive behavior. When possible, the technique also ought to direct the student to the appropriate behavior, such as when a student is escorted to a seat or the student's hand is moved from a neighbor's desk and back to her own paper.

When using touch interference, it is important to be aware of its limitations and possible negative outcomes. Certain students construe any touch by the teacher as an aggressive act and react with aggressive behavior. On one occasion we saw a teacher calmly walk up to a student who was standing at her

30

seat and place her hand on the student's shoulder. The student turned around and confronted the teacher, angrily yelling, "Don't you ever put your hands on me!" To lessen the chance of such an occurrence, teachers need to be sensitive to using touch interference when working with visibly angry or upset students and older students, especially those of the opposite sex. As with all management techniques, the teacher must be cognizant of the situational variables as well as the student characteristics.

Classroom Verbal Intervention

There are four advantages to using nonverbal intervention whenever possible: (1) disruption to the learning process is less likely to occur; (2) hostile confrontation with the student is less apt to happen; (3) the student is provided the opportunity to correct his own behavior before more teacher-centered, public interventions are employed; and (4) a maximum number of remaining alternative interventions is preserved. However, nonverbal intervention is not always possible. When misbehavior is potentially harmful to any student or potentially disruptive for a large number of students, it should be stopped quickly, and often verbal intervention is the quickest way to do so. Before discussing specific techniques, there are some guidelines teachers should keep in mind when using verbal intervention.

1. Whenever possible, use nonverbal interventions first.
2. Keep verbal intervention as private as possible. This minimizes the risk of having the student become defensive and hostile to avoid losing face in front of peers. Brophy (1988) suggests that this is one of the most important general principles for disciplinary intervention.
3. Make the verbal intervention as brief as possible. Your goal is to stop the misbehavior and redirect the student to appropriate behavior. Prolonging the verbal interaction extends the disruption of learning and enhances the likelihood of a hostile confrontation.
4. As Haim Ginott (1972) suggests, speak to the situation, not the person. In other words, label the behavior as bad or inappropriate, not the person. If, for example, a student interrupts a teacher, "Interrupting others is rude" is a more appropriate response than "You interrupted me. You are rude." Labeling the behavior helps the student to see the distinction between himself and his behavior, which in turn helps him to understand that it is possible for the teacher to like him but not his behavior. If the student is labeled, he may feel compelled to defend himself. Furthermore, the student may accept the label as part of his self-concept and match the label with inappropriate behavior in the future. This is exactly what Jimmy Dolan decides to do in Case 4.

31

Case 4 • Jimmy, the Little Sneak

Jimmy Dolan is in the sixth grade at Shortfellow School. His teacher, Mr. Gramble, has had a long history of difficulty in dealing with classroom discipline. Jimmy is a fine student who rarely misbehaves. One day, as his back is partially turned to the class, Mr. Gramble notices Jimmy talking to a neighbor. In a flash, Mr. Gramble turns and pounces on Jimmy, who was only asking Craig Rutler for an eraser to correct a mistake in his homework. "So, you're the one who's been causing all the trouble," Mr. Gramble snaps. "You little sneak, and all the time I thought you were one of the few people who never caused trouble in here. Well, Buster, you can bet from now on I'll keep an eagle eye on you. You won't be getting away with any more sneaky behavior in here."

For a week or so, Jimmy goes back to his typical good behavior, but every time something goes wrong or someone misbehaves, Mr. Gramble blames Jimmy. After a week or so of unjust blame, Jimmy decides that he may as well start causing some trouble since he is going to get blamed for it anyway. In a very short time, Jimmy truly is a great sneak who causes all sorts of havoc and rarely gets caught in the act.

5. As Ginott has urged, set limits on behavior, not on feelings. For instance, tell the student, "It is O.K. to be angry, but it's not O.K. to show your anger by hitting." "It is O.K. to feel disappointed but it's not O.K. to show that disappointment by ripping your test paper up in front of this class and throwing it in the basket." Students need to recognize, trust, and understand their feelings. When teachers and parents tell students not to be angry or disappointed, they are telling them to distrust and deny their genuine and often justified feelings. The appropriate message for teachers and parents to communicate and understand is that there are appropriate and inappropriate ways for expressing feelings.

6. Avoid sarcasm and other verbal behaviors that belittle or demean the student. Using verbal reprimands to belittle students lowers self-esteem and creates sympathy among classmates.

7. Begin by using a technique that fits the student and the problem and is as close as possible to the student-control end of the decision-making hierarchy.

8. If the first verbal intervention does not result in a return to appropriate behavior, use a second technique that is closer to the teacher-control end of the hierarchy.

9. If more than one verbal intervention technique has been used unsuccessfully, it is time to move to the next step of the management hierarchy—the use of logical consequences.

Some ineffective verbal interventions encourage inappropriate behavior. For instance, "I dare you to do that again" actually increases the likelihood that a student will accept the dare and engage in further disruptions. Other verbal interventions focus on irrelevant behavior. "Aren't you sorry for what you did?" or "Why don't you just admit you have a problem?" address issues that are tangential to the real problem, the student's inappropriate behavior. Still other inappropriate interventions give abstract, meaningless directions or predictions, such as, "Grow up!" or "You'll never amount to anything." These do not address the disruptive behavior and are derogatory and humiliating. They increase the possibility of further confrontation when the student attempts to "save face."

FIGURE 1 *Hierarchy of Classroom Verbal Intervention Techniques*

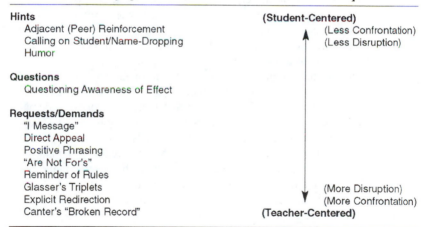

Hints   **(Student-Centered)**
  Adjacent (Peer) Reinforcement   (Less Confrontation)
  Calling on Student/Name-Dropping   (Less Disruption)
  Humor

Questions
  Questioning Awareness of Effect

Requests/Demands
  "I Message"
  Direct Appeal
  Positive Phrasing
  "Are Not For's"
  Reminder of Rules
  Glasser's Triplets   (More Disruption)
  Explicit Redirection   (More Confrontation)
  Canter's "Broken Record"   **(Teacher-Centered)**

With the guidelines in mind and a cognizance of ineffective verbal reactions, let's turn our attention to the hierarchy of effective verbal intervention. Remember that this is a hierarchy of decision making that begins with verbal interventions that foster student control over student behavior and gradually progresses to interventions that foster greater teacher management over student behavior. The teacher uses the hierarchy as a range of options to consider, not as a series of techniques to be tried in rapid succession. The teacher should begin the intervention at the point on the hierarchy that is likely to correct the misbehavior and still allow the student as much control and responsibility as possible. It is entirely appropriate to begin with a teacher-centered technique if the teacher believes that it is important to stop the misbehavior quickly and that only a teacher-centered intervention will do so. It is also important to remember that not all of these interventions are appropriate for all types of misbehavior or for all students. Lasley (1989) suggests that teacher-centered interventions are more appropriate for younger, developmentally immature children, and student-centered interventions are more appropriate for older, developmentally mature learners. Therefore, the effective use of this verbal intervention hierarchy requires the teacher to decide which particular intervention techniques are appropriate for both his students and the particular types of misbehavior that are occurring.

As Figure 1 indicates, the verbal intervention hierarchy has been broken into three major categories: hints, questions, and requests or demands. Hints are indirect means of letting the student know that his behavior is inappropriate. They do not directly address the behavior itself. Thus, of all the verbal interventions, they provide the greatest student control over behavior and are the least likely to result in further disruption or confrontation. Specific techniques that are classified as hints include adjacent or peer reinforcement, calling on students or name dropping, and humor.

Questions are used by the teacher to ask the student if he is aware of how he is behaving and how that behavior is affecting other people. They are more direct than hints but provide greater student control and less likelihood of confrontation than demands. The only questioning technique that is illustrated as such is questioning awareness of effect. However, almost any request or demand can be utilized as a question. For example, "pencils are not for drumming" can be rephrased as "what are pencils for?"

The third level of verbal intervention is labeled as requests/demands. These are teacher statements explicitly directed at a misbehavior that make clear that the teacher wants the inappropriate behavior stopped. Requests and demands exert greater teacher management over student behavior and have the potential to be disruptive and confrontational. Despite their disadvantages, it is sometimes necessary for teachers to use these interventions when lower level interventions have proved unsuccessful. The potential for confrontation can be minimized if the demands are delivered calmly, privately, and assertively rather than aggressively.

No matter which interventions a teacher employs, they must be used with full awareness of their limitations and of the implicit message about managing student behavior that each one conveys.

Adjacent (Peer) Reinforcement

This technique is based on the learning principle that behavior that is reinforced is more likely to be repeated. While usually reinforcement consists of reinforcing a student for his own behavior, Albert Bandura (1977) has demonstrated through his work on social learning theory that other students are likely to imitate an appropriate behavior when their peers have been reinforced for that behavior. The use of peer reinforcement as a verbal intervention technique focuses class attention on appropriate behavior rather than on inappropriate behavior. This intervention technique has been placed first in the hierarchy because it gives the student a chance to control his own behavior without any intervention on the part of the teacher that calls attention to the student or his behavior. Adjacent reinforcement not only can stop misbehavior but also can prevent other students from misbehaving.

To use this technique effectively, a teacher who notes a disruptive behavior finds another student who is behaving appropriately and commends that student publicly for the appropriate behavior. Read Case 5 and notice Mr. Hensen's anger at John. Mr. Hensen could have handled the problem by saying, "Fred and Bob, I really appreciate your raising your hands to answer questions," or "I am really glad that most of us remember the rule that we must raise our hands before speaking."

Case 5 • **Blowing His Stack**

"John, you are one of the most obnoxious students I have ever had the misfortune to deal with. How many times have I asked you not to call out answers? If you want to answer a question, raise your hand. It shouldn't tax your tiny brain too much to remember that. I'm sick and tired of your mistaken idea that the rules of this classroom apply to everyone but you. It's because of people like you that we need rules in the first place. They apply especially to you. I will not allow you to deprive other students of the chance to answer questions. Anyway, half of your answers are totally off the wall.

I'm in charge here, not you. If you don't like it, you can tell your troubles to the principal. Now sit here and be quiet."

When Mr. Hensen finished his lecture and turned to walk to the front of the room, John discreetly flipped him the "bird" and laughed with his friends. John spent the rest of the period drawing pictures on the corner of his desk. The other students spent the remainder of the period in either uncomfortable silence or invisible laughter. Mr. Hensen spent the rest of the class trying to calm down and get his mind back on the lesson.

This particular verbal intervention technique is more useful at the elementary level than at the secondary level. Younger students are usually more interested in pleasing the teacher than older students and often vie for the teacher's attention. Thus, public praise by the teacher is a powerful reinforcer of appropriate behavior. At the secondary level, peer approval is more highly valued than teacher approval; thus, public praise by the teacher is not a powerful reinforcer and indeed may not be a reinforcer at all. For these reasons, it is best to use public praise of individuals sparingly. Public reinforcement of the group as a whole, however, may be an appropriate intervention at the secondary level.

Calling on the Student/Name-Dropping

Using this technique, the teacher redirects the student to appropriate behavior by calling on the student to answer a question or by inserting the student's name in an example or in the middle of a lecture if asking a question is not appropriate. Rinne (1984) labels the technique of inserting the student's name within the content of a lecture "name-dropping." Hearing his name is a good reminder to a student that his attention should be focused on the lesson. This technique may be used to redirect students who are off task but are not disrupting the learning of others (see Chapter 7), as well as students who are overtly disrupting the learning process.

Calling on a student who is misbehaving is a subtle yet effective technique for recapturing the student's attention without interrupting the flow of the lesson or risking confrontation with the student. There are two possible formats for calling on disruptive students. Some teachers state the student's name first and then ask a question; others ask the question and then call on the student. The latter technique invariably results in the student being unable to answer the question because he did not hear it. Often, the teacher who uses this technique follows the period of embarrassed silence with a comment on why the student can't answer and why it is important to pay attention. Although this procedure may satisfy the teacher's need to say, "I gotcha," it is preferable to call on the student first and then ask the question. Using the name first achieves the goal of redirecting the student's attention without embarrassing him.

In Case 5, calling on John to answer or saying John's name are not appropriate techniques for Mr. Hensen to use in dealing with the situation because they encourage John's calling out by giving him recognition. Although not appropriate in this particular case, calling on the student and name-dropping are appropriate in a wide range of situations with learners of all ages.

Humor

Humor that is directed at the teacher or at the situation rather than at the student can defuse tension in the classroom and redirect students to appropriate behavior. The use of humor tends to depersonalize situations and can help to establish positive relationships with students (Saphier and Gower, 1982).

If Mr. Hensen wished to use humor to handle John's calling out, he might say something like this: "I must be hallucinating or something. I'd swear I heard somebody say something if I didn't know for sure that I haven't called on anyone yet." In using this technique, teachers need to be very careful not to turn humor into sarcasm. There is a fine line between humor and sarcasm. Used as a verbal intervention, humor is directed at or makes fun of the teacher or the situation, whereas sarcasm is directed at or makes fun of the student. It is important to keep this distinction in mind to ensure that what is intended as humor does not turn into sarcasm.

Questioning Awareness of Effect

Sometimes students who disrupt learning are genuinely not aware of the effect their behavior has on other people. Our research (Levin, Nolan, and Hoffman, 1985) indicates that even students who are chronic discipline problems learn to control their behavior when they are forced to acknowledge both its positive and negative effects. Given this, making disruptive students aware of how their behavior affects other people can be a powerful technique for getting them to control their own behavior. Usually a teacher can make a student aware of the impact of his behavior through the use of a rhetorical question, which requires no response from the disruptive student. The teacher who wants to handle Mr. Hensen's problem by questioning the student's awareness of his behavior's effect might say something like this: "John, are you aware that your calling out answers without raising your hand robs other students of the chance to answer the question?" As soon as the question was asked, the teacher would continue with the lesson without giving John an opportunity to respond.

The informal question not only makes the student aware of the impact of his behavior but also communicates to other students the teacher's desire to protect their right to learn and may build peer support for appropriate behavior. In using this intervention, however, especially with students at the junior high level or above, the teacher must be prepared for the possibility that the student will respond to the question. If the student does respond and does so in a negative way, the teacher may choose to ignore the answer, thereby sending the message that he will not use class time to discuss the issue; or the teacher may respond, "John, your behavior is having a negative impact on other people, and so I will not permit you to continue calling out answers." This option sends the message that the teacher is in charge of the classroom and will not tolerate the misbehavior. In dealing with a possible negative response from the student, it is important to remember that the teacher's goal is to stop the misbehavior and redirect the student to appropriate behavior as quickly as possible. Prolonged confrontations frustrate that goal.

Sending an "I Message"

Thomas Gordon (1989), the author of Teaching Children Self-Discipline at Home and in School, has developed a useful technique for dealing with misbehavior verbally. He terms the intervention an "I message." The "I message" is a three-part message that is intended to help the disruptive student recognize the negative impact of his behavior on the teacher. The underlying assumption of the technique is the same as the assumption underlying the previously discussed "questioning awareness of effect": Once a student recognizes the negative impact of his behavior on others, he will be motivated to stop the misbehavior. The three parts of an "I message" are (1) a simple description of the disruptive behavior, (2) a description of its tangible effect on the teacher and/or other students, and (3) a description of the teacher's feelings about the effects of the misbehavior. Using "I messages" models for students the important behavior of taking responsibility for and owning one's behavior and feelings. There is one important caveat in the use of this technique. Just as the teacher expects students to respect the feelings that are expressed in an "I message," the teacher must respect feelings expressed by students.

To use an "I message" to stop John from calling out, Mr. Hensen might say, "John, when you call out answers without raising your hand (part 1), I can't call on any other student to answer the question (part 2). This disturbs me because I would like to give everyone a chance to answer the questions (part 3)." Teachers who enjoy a positive relationship with students, which gives them referent power, are usually successful in using "I messages." When students genuinely like the teacher, they are motivated to stop behavior that has a negative impact on the teacher. On the other hand, if the teacher has a poor relationship with students, he should avoid the use of "I messages." Allowing students who dislike you to know that a particular behavior is annoying or disturbing may result in an increase in that particular behavior.

Direct Appeal

Another technique that is useful for instances when a teacher enjoys a referent or expert power base is direct appeal. Direct appeal means courteously requesting that a student stop the disruptive behavior. For example, Mr. Hensen could say, "John, please stop calling out answers so that everyone will have a chance to answer." The direct appeal is not made in any sort of pleading or begging way.

Teachers must not use direct appeal in a classroom in which students seem to doubt the teacher's ability to be in charge. In this situation, the appeal may be perceived as a plea rather than as a straightforward request.

Positive Phrasing

Many times parents and teachers fall into the trap of emphasizing the negative outcomes of misbehavior more than the positive outcomes of appropriate behavior. We tell children and students far more frequently what will happen if they don't finish their homework than we tell them the good things that will occur if they do finish. Of course, it is often easier to identify the short-range negative outcomes of misbehavior than it is to predict the short-range positive impact of appropriate behavior. Still, when the positive outcomes of appropriate behavior are easily identifiable, simply stating what the positive outcomes are, can redirect students from disruptive to proper behavior. Shrigley (1985) has called this technique positive phrasing. It usually takes the form of "as soon as you do X (behave appropriately), we can do Y (a positive outcome)."

In using positive phrasing to correct John's calling out, Mr. Hensen might say, "John, you will be called on as soon as you raise your hand." The long-term advantage of using positive phrasing whenever possible is that students begin to believe that appropriate behavior leads to positive outcomes. As a result, they are more likely to develop internalized control over their behavior.

"Are Not For's"

Of all the verbal interventions discussed in this chapter, the phrase "are not for" (Shrigley, 1985) is the most limited in use. It is implemented primarily when elementary or preschool children misuse property or materials. For example, if a student is drumming on a desk with a pencil, the teacher may say, "Pencils aren't for drumming on desks; pencils are for writing." Although it is usually effective in redirecting behavior positively at the elementary or preschool level, most secondary students perceive this intervention as insulting. Using "are not for" is not an appropriate technique for Mr. Hensen since John is a secondary student and is not misusing property or material.

Reminder of the Rules

When a teacher has established clear guidelines or rules early in the year and has received student commitment to them, merely reminding disruptive students of the rules may curb misbehavior. If past transgressions have been followed by a reminder and a negative logical consequence if the misbehavior continued, this approach is even more effective. Notice that at this point on the hierarchy, the teacher is no longer relying on the student's ability to control his own behavior but instead is using external rules to manage behavior.

In using this technique, Mr. Hensen might say, "John, the classroom rules state that students must raise their hands before speaking," or "John, calling out answers without raising your hand is against our classroom rules." The technique is particularly effective for elementary students and for junior high students. Although it may be used at the senior high level, at this level many students resent the feeling that they are being governed by too many rules. It is important to note that when a reminder of the rules does not redirect the misbehavior, the application of consequences must follow. If this does not occur, the effectiveness of rule reminders will be diminished because students will not see the link between breaking classroom rules and negative consequences.

Glasser's Triplets

In his system for establishing suitable student behavior, which is outlined in Schools Without Failure (1969), William Glasser proposed that teachers direct students to appropriate behavior through the use of three questions: (1) What are you doing? (2) Is it against the rules? (3) What should you be doing? The use of these questions, which are known as Glasser's triplets, obviously requires a classroom in which the rules have been firmly established in students' minds. To stop John from calling out answers, Mr. Hensen would simply ask Glasser's triplets. The expectation underlying Glasser's triplets is that the student will answer the questions honestly and will then return to the appropriate behavior. Unfortunately, not all students answer the triplets honestly, and therein lies the intervention's inherent weakness. Asking open-ended questions may result in student responses that are dishonest, improper, or unexpected.

If a student chooses to answer the questions dishonestly or not to reply at all, the teacher responds by saying (in John's case), "No, John, you were calling out answers. That is against our classroom rules. You must raise your hand to answer questions." To minimize the likelihood of an extended, negative confrontation ensuing from the use of Glasser's triplets, it is suggested that teachers use three statements instead of questions: "John, you are calling out. It is against the rules. You should raise your hand if you want to answer."

Explicit Redirection

Explicit redirection consists of an order to stop the misbehavior and return to acceptable behavior. The redirection is a teacher command and leaves no room for student rebuttal. If Mr. Hensen used explicit redirection with John, he might say, "John, stop calling out answers and raise your hand if you want to answer a question." Notice the contrast between this technique and those discussed in the earlier stages of the hierarchy in terms of the amount of responsibility the teacher assumes for managing student behavior.

The advantages of this technique are its simplicity, clarity, and closed format, which does not allow for student rebuttal. Its disadvantage lies in the fact that the teacher publicly confronts the student, who either behaves or defies the teacher in front of peers. Obviously, if the student chooses to defy the teacher's command, the teacher must be prepared to proceed to the next step in the hierarchy and enforce the command with appropriate consequences.

Canter's "Broken Record"

Lee Canter (1992) has developed a strategy for clearly communicating to the student that the teacher will not engage in verbal bantering and intends to make sure that the student resumes appropriate behavior. Canter has labeled his strategy "the broken record" because the teacher's behavior sounds like a broken record. The teacher begins by giving the student an explicit redirection statement. If the student doesn't comply or if the student tries to defend or explain his behavior, the teacher repeats the redirection. The teacher may repeat it two or three times if the student continues to argue or fails to comply. If the student tries to excuse or defend his behavior, some teachers add the phrase "that's not the point" at the beginning of the first and second repetitions. The following is an example of this technique as applied by Mr. Hensen.

> **Hensen:** "John, stop calling out answers and raise your hand if you want to answer questions."
> **John:** "But I really do know the answer."
> **Hensen:** "That's not the point. Stop calling out answers and raise your hand if you want to answer questions."
> **John:** "You let Mabel call out answers yesterday."
> **Hensen:** "That's not the point. Stop calling out answers and raise your hand if you want to answer questions."
> Return to lesson.

We have found the "broken record" technique to be very good for avoiding verbal battles with students. If, however, the statement has been repeated three times without any result, it is probably time to move to a stronger measure, such as the application of logical consequences.

Comply or Face the Logical Consequences: "You Have a Choice"

Although nonverbal and verbal interventions often stop misbehavior, sometimes the misbehavior remains unchecked. When this occurs, the teacher needs to use more overt techniques. The final tier on the decision-making management hierarchy is the use of logical consequences to manage student behavior.

When nonverbal and verbal interventions have not led to appropriate behavior, the teacher must take control of the situation and use logical consequences to manage student behavior. To do so, the teacher applies logical consequences calmly and thoughtfully in a forceful but not punitive manner.

Brophy (1988) suggests that the teacher who uses logical consequences should emphasize the student changing his behavior rather than retribution. When this is done, the teacher makes sure that the student understands the misbehavior must stop immediately or negative consequences will result. Often it is effective to give the student a choice of either complying with the request or facing the consequence. This technique is called "You Have a Choice." For example, if John continued to call out answers after Mr. Hensen had tried several nonverbal and verbal interventions, Mr. Hensen would say, "John, you have a choice. Stop calling out answers immediately and begin raising your hand to answer or move your seat to the back of the room and you and I will have a private discussion later. You decide." Phrasing the intervention in this way helps the student to realize that he is responsible for the positive as well as the negative consequences of his behavior and that the choice is his. It also places the teacher in a neutral rather than punitive role. Remember, students do, in fact, choose how to behave. Teachers can't control student behavior; they can only influence it.

Obviously the exact consequence to be applied varies with the student misbehavior. However, one principle is always involved in the formulation of consequences: The consequence should be as directly related to the offense as possible. Consistent application of this principle helps students to recognize that their behavior has consequences and helps them learn to control their own behavior in the future by predicting its consequences beforehand.

Because it can be difficult to come up with directly related logical consequences on the spur of the moment (Canter, 1992), teachers should consider logical consequences for common types of misbehavior before the misbehaviors occur. When misbehavior occurs for which there is no preplanned logical consequence, a teacher should ask the following questions to help formulate a consequence directly related to the misbehavior:

1. What would be the logical result if this misbehavior went unchecked?
2. What are the direct effects of this behavior on the teacher, other students, and the misbehaving student?
3. What can be done to minimize these effects?

The answers to these three questions usually will help a teacher to identify a logical consequence. The ideas presented in this chapter constitute a complete hierarchy that teachers can use to guide their thinking and decision making concerning interventions to cope with classroom misbehavior. The hierarchy is presented in its complete format in Figure 2.

Figure 2   Hierarchy for Management Intervention

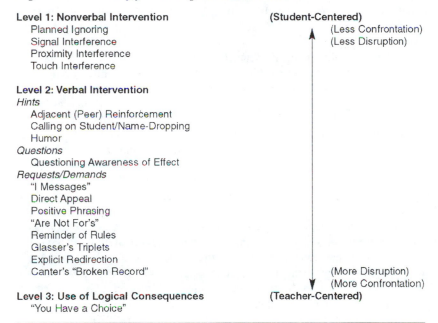

Level 1: Nonverbal Intervention   **(Student-Centered)**
    Planned Ignoring   (Less Confrontation)
    Signal Interference   (Less Disruption)
    Proximity Interference
    Touch Interference

Level 2: Verbal Intervention
Hints
    Adjacent (Peer) Reinforcement
    Calling on Student/Name-Dropping
    Humor
Questions
    Questioning Awareness of Effect
Requests/Demands
    "I Messages"
    Direct Appeal
    Positive Phrasing
    "Are Not For's"
    Reminder of Rules
    Glasser's Triplets
    Explicit Redirection
    Canter's "Broken Record"   (More Disruption)
                                                         (More Confrontation)
Level 3: Use of Logical Consequences   **(Teacher-Centered)**
    "You Have a Choice"

IV. MANAGING CHRONIC MISBEHAVIOR PROBLEMS

Relationship Building

Without a doubt, the development of a positive relationship between the teacher and the student with a chronic behavior problem is one of the most effective strategies for helping such students. Usually these students do not have positive relationships with their teachers. Indeed, teachers often tend to avoid interaction with such students. This is quite understandable. Students who have chronic behavior problems are often difficult to deal with. They disrupt the carefully planned learning activities of the teacher. They sometimes intimidate other students and prevent their peers from engaging in classroom activities. They frequently challenge the teacher's authority and cause the teacher to doubt her own competence.

These doubts about competence arise from the misconception that the teacher can control a student's behavior. The teacher can only influence a student's behavior and can react to that behavior. She cannot control anyone's behavior except her own. If a teacher has the mistaken notion that her job is to control a student's behavior, she will feel that she is not as competent as she should be every time the student acts inappropriately. Thus, one of the first steps a teacher should take in working with students who have chronic behavior problems is to recognize that her role is to help these students learn to control their own behavior. The teacher can only be held accountable for controlling her own behavior in such a way that it increases the likelihood that the students will learn and want to behave appropriately.

To accomplish this, the teacher must disregard any negative feelings she has toward the chronically disruptive student and work at building a positive relationship with that student. Understand that we are not suggesting that the teacher must like the student. This is not always possible. No teacher honestly likes every student whom she has ever encountered. However, a truly professional teacher does not act on or reveal those negative feelings.

Our experience has given us two important insights about working with students who have chronic behavior problems. First, teachers who look for and are able to find some positive qualities, no matter how small or how hidden, in chronically disruptive students are much more successful in helping those students learn to behave appropriately than those who do not. Second, the primary factor that motivated the vast majority of students who were at one time chronically disruptive to turn their behavior around was the development of a close, positive relationship with some caring adult. Case 6 illustrates the impact that a caring relationship can have on such an individual.

Case 6 • Darnell

Darnell, who was born to a single mother in a rundown, crime-ridden neighborhood, was raised by his grandmother, the one kind, caring, and protective figure in his early life. Despite her efforts to shield him, Darnell was exposed to drugs, street violence, and a variety of illegal activity while he was still in elementary school. In middle school, Darnell, who describes himself at that age as full of anger and energy, became involved in petty theft and violent attacks on other adolescents and adults. As a result, he was sent to a juvenile detention facility and, after his release, assigned to Barbara, a juvenile probation officer.

Barbara was a streetwise veteran in her fifties who had worked with many troubled adolescents. As Darnell has said, "She did not take any crap." Barbara insisted that Darnell stop his aggressive behavior. She made it clear to him that she saw him as an intelligent young man who had the potential to be successful if he changed his behavior. Over the six-year period Darnell and Barbara worked together, Darnell changed dramatically. In Darnell's words,

"Barbara taught me how to take my anger and my aggression and turn them into positive forces, first on the basketball court and then later, much later in the classroom." As a result of the close, positive relationship Barbara built, Darnell earned passing grades in school, stayed out of trouble, and became a good enough point guard to earn a scholarship to a small state college. He became a special education teacher and returned to his home to teach, hoping to make a difference in the lives of kids like him.

After returning, he saw the need to change the educational system itself but felt powerless to do so. After a few frustrating years, he left teaching and went on to earn a master's degree in counseling, a Ph.D. in curriculum, and a principal's certificate. Today, Darnell is a middle-school principal in the inner city where he was raised. He lives in the city with his wife and young son and spends his time helping inner city kids turn their energy and anger to useful purposes in much the same way as Barbara helped him.

Of course, building positive relationships with students who have chronic behavior problems is not always an easy task. Many students with chronic behavior problems have a long history of unsuccessful relationships with adults. Because the adults in these relationships have ended up being abusive in one way or another, many of the students actively resist attempts to build positive relationships. Brendtro, Brokenleg, and Van Bockern (1990) suggest that the teacher who works with students with chronic behavior problems should think of the student's natural desire to form attachments with significant others as if it were a piece of masking tape and the significant others were walls. Each time the student begins to form a relationship with an adult, the masking tape sticks to the wall. Each time the relationship ends in a negative or hurtful way, the masking tape is ripped off the wall. This process of attachment and hurt is repeated several times. Eventually, the masking tape stops sticking. In other words, the desire to form attachments and relationships with adults is lost. In the eyes of the student, it becomes safer not to build any relationships at all than to risk another relationship that will result in hurt and disappointment.

Thus, teachers who want to build relationships with such students must be persistent, consistent, and predictable in their own behavior toward the student. They must search for positive qualities in the students and work at building the relationship without much initial encouragement or response from the student. As Brendtro, Brokenleg, and Van Bockern note, the desire to build a relationship does not have to spring from a feeling of liking or attraction. The teacher simply has to choose to act toward the student in caring and giving ways. Over time, positive feelings of liking and attraction develop. Notice how Carol, the student teacher in Case 7, slowly builds a relationship with Cindy. Although such dramatic results do not always or even typically occur, the efforts can be rewarding.

Case 7 • Relating to Cindy

Carol, a student teacher in chemistry, decided to make Cindy "her project." Cindy was an overweight, physically unattractive junior who did not seem to have any friends at all. She spoke to no one, did not participate in class activities, and had failed every test and quiz from September to late January when Carol took over the class.

Every day in the four minutes before class began, Carol walked back to Cindy's desk and tried to chat with her. For two full weeks Carol got absolutely no response, not even eye contact. Cindy completely ignored her. Although upset and disappointed, Carol decided to persist. One day during the third week without a response, Carol noticed Cindy reading the college newspaper during class. Instead of viewing this as a discipline problem, Carol decided to use it as the foundation for a relationship. She had Cindy stay after class and told her that she had seen the newspaper. She asked if Cindy was

interested in newspapers. Cindy replied that she wanted to be a journalist. Carol told Cindy she would be happy to bring her a copy of the college newspaper every day as long as Cindy would read it after class. For the first time Cindy replied, saying, "That would be great."

Everyday for the next ten weeks, Carol drove fifteen minutes out of her way to pick up a newspaper for Cindy. The impact on Cindy was remarkable. She began coming to class early and staying after class each day to speak with Carol. She attended class activities and even participated verbally about once a week or so. Remarkably, she passed every test and quiz from that point until Carol's student teaching experience ended. Given the cumulative nature of the content of chemistry, this academic turnaround astounded Carol, her supervisor (one of the authors), and her cooperating teacher.

46

Bob Strachota (1996) calls attempts to build positive relationships with students who have chronic behavior problems "getting on their side." He notes that teachers need to view themselves as allies rather than opponents of these students and has suggested several steps to help teachers do so. The first step is "wondering why." Strachota points out that many teachers become so preoccupied with techniques for stopping the misbehavior that they forget to ask such fundamental questions as (1) why is the student behaving in this way? and (2) what purpose does it serve or what need does it fulfill? Strachota's underlying assumption is that behavior is purposeful rather than random and directed at meeting some need even if the goal of the behavior is faulty or mistaken. If the teacher can identify the need, it is often possible to substitute a positive behavior that will result in fulfillment of the need.

The second step is to develop a sense of empathy and intimacy with the student. Have you ever found yourself in a situation in which you wanted to stop a behavior but couldn't get control of it? Have you ever yelled at your children using the same words as your parents despite your promise to yourself that would never happen? Have you ever eaten too much or had too much to drink although you vowed that you wouldn't? If you have, then you have a great opportunity to develop a sense of empathy with these students. If you can view yourself and the student in similar terms—wanting to stop a behavior but not being able to—you are much more likely to be able to work successfully with the student.

The third step is to stay alert for cues and behaviors that reveal other aspects of the student's personality. Sometimes teachers become so riveted on the misbehavior that they do not look at other aspects of the student's behavior and personality. Students who pose chronic behavior problems have other aspects to their beings as well, but it takes self-control and persistence to focus on them. When a teacher is controlled and focused enough to see the student's personality and behavior in its entirety, she is often able to find positive and attractive aspects that can be used as a foundation for building a positive relationship.

Strachota's fourth and final step is for the teacher to monitor carefully her own behavior in interacting with the student. Strachota points out, "What's going on for me leaks out in the way I talk. I know what I sound like when I am happy, relaxed, curious, flexible, enthusiastic, etc. I know the difference when I feel tense, short, angry, controlling, hurried, sarcastic, or harsh" (1996, p. 75). Sometimes teachers unintentionally communicate negative feelings toward disruptive and low-achieving students. If a teacher listens closely to what she is saying and observes how she is behaving, she can avoid negative messages and instead offer positive, caring ones.

Our experience reinforces Strachota's belief that the teacher's mindset is critical. In most chronic behavior situations, the teacher sees the student as an opponent in the conflict. Teachers who are successful in resolving chronic behavior problems see themselves on the student's side, working together to overcome the problem.

Breaking the Cycle of Discouragement

Many students with chronic behavior problems suffer from low self-esteem and have a low success-to-failure. Their need for a sense of significance or belonging, a sense of competence or mastery, a sense of power or independence, and a sense of virtue or generosity have not been fulfilled. When these needs are not fulfilled, individuals take action to fulfill them. Unfortunately, the student with chronic behavior problems often takes actions that are inappropriate and negative. These negative behaviors are met with negative teacher responses, punishments, and consequences that further reduce the student's self-esteem and lead to further misbehavior, negative responses, punishments, and consequences. This cycle of discouragement, which is depicted in Figure 3, will continue until a teacher takes action to break it.

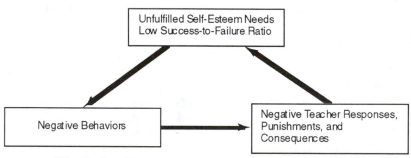

Figure 3 The Cycle of Discouragement

Although it is entirely appropriate for these students to receive negative messages about their inappropriate behavior and to experience the negative consequences of such actions, if that is all that occurs, the cycle of discouragement is simply reinforced. Suppose after reading this chapter, you walked into your kitchen and saw water pouring from underneath your kitchen sink. What would you do? While you might prefer to close the kitchen door, pretend you never saw it, and go golfing, that would not be the appropriate adult response. The appropriate response would be to shut off the water and then fix the leak. Shutting off the water is like applying punishment or consequences. It stops the water (the inappropriate behavior), but it does not fix the leak (the unfulfilled self-esteem needs). While it is necessary to stop the misbehavior, the teacher must also find ways to meet those unfulfilled needs and break the cycle of discouragement.

Just as there are students who are caught in the cycle of discouragement, there are students who are caught in the cycle of encouragement. These students have a high success-to-failure ratio and are having their needs for feelings of significance, competence, power, and virtue met. As a result, they behave in positive and caring ways toward teachers and peers. These positive behaviors are reciprocated, and students are given the message that they are attractive, competent and virtuous, resulting in a cycle of encouragement. We believe that the appropriate way to solve chronic behavior problems is to break the cycle of discouragement by stopping the inappropriate behavior through management techniques and, at the same time, engaging in behaviors that will help to meet the student's needs for feelings of significance, competence, power, and virtue. Together, these two actions result in the disruption of the cycle of discouragement.

To accomplish this, teachers who are dealing with students with chronic behavior problems should ask themselves four questions:

1. What can I do to help meet this student's need for significance or belonging?
2. What can I do to help meet this student's need for competence or mastery?
3. What can I do to help meet this student's need for power or independence?
4. What can I do to help meet this student's need for virtue or generosity?

Obviously, suggestions that follow are not the only possibilities. We know that teachers will use their own creativity to build upon and enhance these ideas.

At the elementary level, it is sometimes effective to place the student with chronic behavior problems in a responsible role, for example, message carrier. This often enhances the student's sense of belonging. In middle school and high school finding clubs, intramurals, or other extracurricular activities or out-of-school activities (sometimes a job) in which the student has some interest and talent and then supporting the student's participation in this activity helps to enhance the student's sense of belonging. At all levels, the teacher should make it a point to give the student attention and positive feedback when she engages in appropriate behavior.

The need for a sense of competence can be met by the use of encouragement. Often students with chronic behavior problems and their parents receive only negative messages. Showing an interest in those things that the student values and making sure that you, as the teacher, recognize those strengths will help to increase the student's sense of competence. Sometimes setting short-term goals with the student and then helping the student to keep track of his progress in meeting the goals helps the student to feel more competent.

At all times, feedback to the student with chronic behavior problems should emphasize what the student can do as opposed to what the student cannot do. Suppose, for example, that a student with chronic behavior problems takes a valid test of the material the student was supposed to learn, makes a concerted effort to do well, and receives a 67 on the test. In most classrooms, the only message that the student would receive, would be one of failure, which would reinforce the student's own feelings of incompetence. If we examine the situation more objectively, however, we can see that the student knows twice as much as she does not know. This does not mean that 67 is good or acceptable, but rather than communicating that the student is a failure, the teacher can point out that the student has indeed learned and then use that limited success to encourage the student to continue to make the effort to learn. Using encouraging communication, engaging the student in short-term goal setting, stressing effort and improvement, and focusing on the positive aspects of the student's behavior and performance can increase the student's sense of competence.

Before turning to techniques for managing chronic behavior problems, it should be emphasized that relationship building and breaking the cycle of discouragement require commitment, persistence, patience, and self-control on the part of the teacher. These strategies will not turn things around over night. Sometimes they do not result in any tangible benefits for several weeks or months. Persisting with them and ignoring the natural desire to get even or give up constitute the ultimate in professional behavior. It is extremely hard to do, but it is often the only thing that makes a real difference to students with chronic behavior problems in the long run.

Private Conferences

Holding private conferences with students who have chronic behavior problems is the sine qua non of the strategies that are intended to manage or solve these behavior problems. Until the teacher takes the time to sit down with the student to discuss the student's behavior and to attempt to find ways to help the student behave in more productive ways, the teacher has not begun to attempt to manage or solve the problem. A private conference or a series of conferences with the student accomplishes several important tasks. First, it makes sure that the student is aware that her behavior is a problem that must be dealt with. Second, sometimes it is one of the basic steps toward building a positive relationship with the student. Thus, it can be an important step toward helping the student to take ownership of the behavior and find ways to bring it under control.

Receiving Skills

During private conferences, the teacher needs to be aware of the student's perception of the problem and point of view in order to be sure that the intervention focuses on the actual problem. Suppose, for example, the student's chronic misbehavior is motivated by the student's belief that she doesn't have the ability to do the assigned work. Solutions that ignore the student's underlying feeling of incompetence are not likely to be successful in the long run. Therefore, it is important to be sure you receive the message that the student is sending. The following receiving skills will help to ensure that you receive the student's message.

1. *Use silence and nonverbal attending cues.* Allow the student sufficient time to express her ideas and feelings and employ nonverbal cues such as eye contact, facial expressions, head nodding, and body posture (for example, leaning toward the student) to show that you are interested in and listening to what she is saying. Most important, make sure these cues are sincere; that is, that you really are listening carefully to the student.

2. *Probe.* Ask relevant and pertinent questions to elicit extended information about a given topic, for clarification of ideas, and for justification of a given idea. Questions such as "Can you tell me more about the problem with Jerry?" "What makes you say that I don't like you?" "I'm not sure I understand what you mean by hitting on you; can you explain what that means?" show that you are listening and want more information.

3. *Check perceptions.* Paraphrase or summarize what the student has said using slightly different words. This acts as a check on whether you have understood the student correctly. This is not a simple verbatim repetition of what the student has said. It is an attempt by the teacher to capture the student's message as accurately as possible in the teacher's words. Usually a perception check ends by giving the student an opportunity to affirm or negate the teacher's perception; for example, "So, as I understand it, you think that I'm picking on you when I give you detention for not completing your homework; is that right?" or "You're saying that you never really wanted to be in the gifted program anyway, and so you don't care whether you are removed from the program. Do I have that right?"

4. *Check feelings.* Feeling checks refer to attempts to reach student emotions through questions and statements. In formulating the questions and statements, use nonverbal cues (for example, facial expression) and paralingual cues (voice volume, rate, and pitch) to go beyond the student's statements and understand the emotions behind

the words. For instance, "It sounds as if you are really proud of what you're doing in basketball, aren't you?" or "You look really angry when you talk about being placed in the lower section. Are you angry?"

Sending Skills

Individual conferences not only allow the teacher to be sure she understands the problem from the student's vantage point, but also allow the teacher to be sure the student understands the problem from the teacher's point of view. Using sending skills to communicate the teacher's thoughts and ideas clearly is a first step toward helping the student gain that insight. Ginott (1972) and Jones (1980) offer the following guidelines for sending accurate messages:

1. *Deal in the here and now.* Don't dwell on past problems and situations. Communicate your thoughts about the present situation and the immediate future. Although it is appropriate to talk about the past behavior that has created the need for the private conference, there is nothing to be gained by reciting a litany of past transgressions.

2. *Make eye contact and use congruent nonverbal behaviors.* Avoiding eye contact when confronting a student about misbehavior gives the student the impression that you are uncomfortable about the confrontation. In contrast, maintaining eye contact helps to let the student know that you are confident and comfortable in dealing with problems. Because research indicates that students believe the nonverbal message when verbal and nonverbal behavior are not congruent (Woolfolk and Brooks, 1983), be sure nonverbal cues match the verbal messages. Smiling as you tell the student how disappointed you are in her behavior is clearly inappropriate.

3. *Make statements rather than ask questions.* Asking questions is appropriate for eliciting information from the student. However, when the teacher has specific information or behaviors to discuss, the teacher should lay the specific facts out on the table rather than try to elicit them from the student by playing "guess what's on my mind."

4. *Use "I"—take responsibility for your feelings.* You have a right to your feelings. It can be appropriate to be annoyed at students, and it can be appropriate to be proud of students. Sometimes teachers try to disown their feelings and act as if they were robots. Students must know that teachers are people who have legitimate feelings and that their feelings must be considered in determining the effects of the student's behavior on others.

5. *Be brief. Get to the point quickly.* Let the student know what the problem is as you see it and what you propose to do about it. Once you

have done this, stop. Don't belabor the issue with unnecessary lectures and harangues.

6. *Talk directly to the student, not about her.* Even if other people are present, talk to the student rather than to parents or counselors. Use "you" and specifically describe the problem to the student. This behavior sends the student the powerful message that she, not her parents or anyone else, is directly responsible for her own behavior.

7. *Give directions to help the students correct the problem.* Don't stop at identifying the problem behavior. Be specific in setting forth exactly what behaviors must be replaced and in identifying appropriate behaviors to replace them.

8. *Check student understanding of your message.* Once you have communicated clearly what the specific problem is and what steps you suggest for solving it, ask a question to be sure the student has received the message correctly. Often it is a good idea to ask the student to summarize the discussion. If the student's summary indicates that she has missed the message, the teacher has an opportunity to restate or rephrase the main idea in a way that the student can understand.

With these guidelines for effective communication in mind, we can now consider three specific techniques for managing students with chronic behavior problems. There are five assumptions underlying these techniques:

1. The number of students in any one class who should be classified as having chronic behavior problems is small, usually fewer than five. If there are more than five, it is a good indication that the teacher has not done all that could be done to prevent the problems from occurring.

2. The teacher is well prepared for each class, engages the students in interesting learning activities, and employs a variety of effective teaching strategies.

3. The expectations for behavior are clearly understood by students and enforced on a consistent basis.

4. The teacher manages commonplace disruptions with a preplanned hierarchy of nonverbal and verbal interventions and logical consequences.

5. The teacher attempts to build positive relationships with students who have chronic behavior problems and attempts to break the cycle of discouragement by helping them to meet their self-esteem needs.

The teacher who is not aware of these assumptions may use the management techniques that follow ineffectively or inappropriately in a given situation.

53

When there are several students who exhibit chronic behavior problems, they usually fall into one of two categories—those who have the greatest potential for improving their behavior quickly and those whose behavior causes the greatest disruption. When there are several students with chronic behavior problems in one class, the teacher may have to choose to work with one category over another. There are pitfalls in either choice. Usually those with the greatest odds for quick improvement are the students with the least severe behavioral problems. Thus, even if the teacher succeeds in helping them, the general level of disruption in the classroom may remain quite high. On the other hand, those students who have the most severe and most disruptive behavior usually require the longest period of time to improve but their improvement tends to have a more dramatic impact on the classroom.

There are no clear guidelines as to which category of students teachers should choose. It is really a matter of personal preference. If the teacher is the type of individual who needs to see results quickly in order to persist, she is probably better off choosing those students with the greatest likelihood for quick improvement. If, however, the more serious behavior is threatening to any individuals, the teacher must begin intervention with those students.

It must be noted that self-monitoring, anecdotal record keeping, or behavior contracting probably will not be effective in managing chronic behavior problems if the five assumptions underlying these techniques have not been met. If these assumptions have been met, then the teacher has done all that she can do to prevent behavior problems from occurring, and management techniques have a reasonably high chance of success.

Management Techniques

Self-Monitoring

Some students who exhibit chronic disruptive behaviors perceive a well-managed private conference as a sign of a teacher's caring and support. Some students leave the conference with a new understanding that their behaviors are interfering with the rights of others and will no longer be tolerated in the classroom. Given the nature and background of chronic behavioral problems, however, most students will need more intensive and frequent intervention techniques. The challenge is to design techniques that are congruent with the belief that students must be given opportunities to learn how to control their own behavior.

Self-monitoring of behavior is a student-directed approach that is often effective with students who are really trying to behave appropriately but seem to need assistance to do so. The technique is usually more appropriate for elementary students who have extremely short attention spans or who are easily distracted by the everyday events of a busy classroom. While self-monitoring can be effective with some older students, the teacher must consider the age appropriateness of the self-monitoring instrument that the student will use.

For self-monitoring to be effective, the instrument must clearly delineate the behaviors to be monitored and must be easy for a student to use. The student must also clearly understand the duration of the self-monitoring and the frequency of behavioral checks. Unfortunately, teachers occasionally design an instrument that is too cumbersome to use or is too time consuming. Thus, using the instrument actually interferes with on-task behavior.

In the beginning, the student may require teacher cues to indicate when it is time to check behavior and record it on the self-monitoring instrument. These cues may be private, nonverbal signals agreed upon by the teacher and the student. In the beginning, it is a good idea for the teacher to co-monitor the student's behavior using the same instrument. When this is done, the teacher and the student can compare their monitoring consistency and discuss the proper use of the instrument as well as the progress that is being made.

The effectiveness of self-monitoring relies heavily on how the use of the instrument is explained to the student. If self-monitoring is presented as a technique that students can use to help themselves with the teacher's assistance, support, and encouragement, the likelihood of improved behavior is high. When teachers have successfully communicated the purpose of the technique and stressed the possible positive outcomes, students have actually thanked them for the opportunity and means to demonstrate on-task behavior. On the other hand, if the intervention is introduced as a form of punishment, the likelihood of positive behavioral change is diminished.

Figure 4 is an example of a simple self-monitoring instrument for a wide range of behaviors. When a teacher uses this instrument, it is imperative that she and the student clearly understand what behaviors are defined as on task, and therefore coded "1," and what behaviors are off task and coded "0." In addition, a workable coding period needs to be established so that each block represents a predetermined period of time.

Yes = 1							No = 0				
1	2	3	4	5	6	7	8	9	10	11	12

Score = sum of the cells = _____

FIGURE 4 *Am I on Task?*

As with any intervention that focuses on the improvement of chronic behavior, progress may be slow. Two steps forward and one step backward may be the best a student can do in the beginning. We must remember that chronic misbehavior does not develop in a day, and it will not be replaced with more appropriate behavior in a day. It is difficult to learn new behaviors to replace behaviors that have become ingrained and habitual. Therefore, the teacher must be patient and focus on improvements. It is usually best to work on one behavior at a time. For example, if a student continually talks to neighbors and calls out, the teacher and student should decide on which behavior to work on first. If the student is successful in managing the selected behavior, experience has shown that subsequent behaviors are more readily corrected.

As behavior improves, the teacher should begin to wean the student from self-monitoring. As a first step, once the teacher is convinced that the student is reliably monitoring her own behavior, the teacher stops co-monitoring and relies solely on the student's report. Next, as behaviors begin to improve, the teacher lengthens the period of time between self-checks. Finally, the teacher removes the student completely from self-monitoring. When this happens, the teacher uses the event to build self-esteem and self-control by making the student aware that she has changed her behavior on her own and should be quite proud of her accomplishments. Any corresponding improvements in academics or peer interactions should also be noted and tied to the student's improved behavior.

Figure 5 is a checklist that teachers can use to evaluate the self-monitoring procedures and instruments that they design.

FIGURE 5 *Self-Monitoring Checklist*

1.	Do the teacher and student clearly understand and agree on the behaviors to be monitored?	_____ Yes	_____No
2	Is the time period for self-checks clearly specified?	_____ Yes	_____No
3.	Does the student understand how to use the instrument?	_____ Yes	_____No
4.	Have the teacher and student agreed on a meeting time to discuss the self-monitoring?	_____ Yes	_____No
5.	Is the instrument designed so that small increments of improved behavior will be noted?	_____ Yes	_____No
6.	Is the instrument designed to focus on one behavior?	_____ Yes	_____No

Anecdotal Record Keeping

If the teacher either has tried self-monitoring or has decided not to try this technique because of philosophical objections or the student's refusal to make the required commitments, there is a second option, called anecdotal record keeping, for remediating chronic behavioral problems. This method, which is a collaborative approach to managing classroom behaviors (see Chapter 4), has been used successfully by student teachers and veteran teachers alike to handle a variety of chronic discipline problems at a variety of grade levels (Levin, Nolan, and Hoffman, 1985). It is based on the principles of Adlerian psychology, which state that changes in behavior can be facilitated by making people aware of their behavior and its consequences for themselves and others (Sweeney, 1981).

Anecdotal record keeping is usually most appropriate for middle and secondary students because students at these levels have better developed self-regulation. To employ the technique, the teacher merely records the classroom behavior, both positive and negative, of a chronically disruptive student over a period of a few weeks. Although it is preferable to have the student's cooperation, anecdotal record keeping can be employed without it.

The record the teacher has made of the student's behavior and the measures that have been taken to improve that behavior form the basis for a private conference with the student. There are nine guidelines that should be followed in conducting this initial conference:

1. The teacher should begin on a positive note.
2. The teacher should help the student to recognize the past behavior and its negative impact, showing the student the record of past behaviors and discussing it if necessary.
3. The teacher should explain that this behavior is unacceptable and must change.
4. The teacher should tell the student that she will keep a record of the student's positive and negative behavior on a daily basis and that the student will be required to sign the record at the end of class each day.
5. The teacher should record the student's home phone number on the top of the record and indicate that she will contact the parents to inform them of continued unacceptable behavior. (This option may not be useful for senior high students because parents are often not as influential at this age.)
6. The teacher should be positive and emphasize expectations of improvement.
7. The conference should be recorded on the anecdotal record.
8. A verbal commitment for improved behavior from the student should be sought. This commitment, or the refusal to give it, should be noted on the anecdotal record.
9. The student should sign the anecdotal record at the end of the conference. If the student refuses to sign, the refusal should be recorded.

After the initial conference, the teacher continues the anecdotal record, each day highlighting positive behaviors, documenting negative behaviors, and noting any corrective measures taken. Keeping this systematic record enables the teacher to focus on the behavior (the deed) rather than on the student (the doer) (Ginott, 1972). The teacher reinforces the student for improved behaviors and, if possible, clarifies the connection between improved behaviors and academic achievement. Thus, the teacher "catches the student being good" (Canter, 1989; Jones, 1980) and demonstrates the concept of encouragement (Dreikurs, Grundwald, and Pepper, 1998). To illustrate the concept of student accountability, the teacher must be consistent in recording behaviors, sharing the record with the student, and obtaining the student's signature on a daily basis (Brophy, 1988). If the student refuses to sign the record on any day, the teacher simply records this fact on the record. Figure 6 is the anecdotal record used with one tenth-grade student over a three-week period. The technique succeeded after the management hierarchy had been utilized with little improvement in the student's behavior. Note that the teacher highlighted positive behaviors to "catch the student being good."

While teachers may think that this technique will consume a lot of instructional time, it does not. If the documentation occurs in the last few minutes of class, perhaps when students are doing homework or getting ready for the next class, the two or three minutes required for it compare favorably to the enormous amount of time wasted by unresolved chronic discipline problems. Thus, this technique actually helps to conserve time by making more efficient use of classroom time.

In studying the use of anecdotal record keeping, Levin, Nolan, and Hoffman (1985) requested teachers to log their views on the effectiveness of the procedure. Here are three representative logs by secondary teachers.

Teacher's Log—Eleventh-Grade English

About a week and a half ago, I implemented the anecdotal record in one of my classes. Two male students were the subjects. The improvement shown by one of these students is very impressive.

On the first day that I held a conference with the student, I explained the procedure, showed him my records for the day, and asked for his signature. He scribbled his name and looked at me as if to say, "What a joke." On the second day, his behavior in class was negative again. This time, when I spoke to him and told him that one more day of disruptive behavior would result in a phone call to his parents, he looked at me as if to say, "This joke isn't so funny anymore." From that moment on, there was a marked improvement in his behavior. He was quiet and attentive in class. After class, he would come up to me and ask me where he was supposed to sign his name for the day. And he "beamed" from my remarks about how well behaved he was that day. Only one time after that did I have to speak to him for negative behavior. I caught him throwing a piece of paper. As soon as he saw me looking at him, he said, "Are you going to write that down in your report?" Then, after class, he came up to me with a worried expression on his face and asked, "Are you going to call my parents?" I didn't because of the previous days of model behavior.

I must say that I was skeptical about beginning this type of record on the students. It seemed like such a lengthy and time-consuming process. But I'll say what I'm feeling now. If the anecdotal record can give positive results more times than not, I'll keep on using it. If you can get one student under control, who is to say you can't get five or ten students under control? It truly is a worthwhile procedure to consider.

Teacher's Log—Tenth-Grade Science
Day 1

As a third or fourth alternative, I used an anecdotal record to help control the discipline problems incurred [sic] in my second-period class. Previously, I had used direct requests or statements (for example, "What are you doing? What should you be doing?" "Your talking is interfering with other students' right to learn," etcetera). The anecdotal record involved having one-to-one conferences with the four students. The conferences were aimed at reviewing the students' classroom behaviors and securing commitments from them for improved behavior. It was fairly successful, as I received a commitment from the four involved; and they, in turn, let the rest of the class in on the deal. In choosing the four students, I tried to pick a student from each trouble pair. Hopefully, this will eliminate misbehavior for both.

Day 2

The progress in my class with the anecdotal records was excellent today, as I expected. The four students were exceptionally well behaved. I will be sure to keep extra-close tabs on their progress the next few days to prevent them from reverting back [sic] to old ways.

FIGURE 6 *Anecdotal Record*

Student's Name _____

Home Phone _____

Date	Student Behavior	Teacher Action	Student Signature
4/14	Talking with Van Out of seat 3 times Refused to answer question	Verbal reprimand Told her to get back Went on	
4/16	Had private conference Rhonda agreed to improve	Explained anecdotal record Was supportive	
4/17	Stayed on task in lab	Positive feedback	
4/20	Late for class Worked quietly	Verbal reminder Positive feedback	
4/21	Worked quietly Wrestling with Jill	Positive feedback Verbal reprimand	
4/22	No disruptions Volunteered to answer	Positive feedback Called on her 3 times	
4/23	Late for class Left without signing	Detention after school Recorded it on record	
4/24	Missed detention	Two days' detention	
4/27	Stayed on task all class	Positive feedback	
4/28	Listened attentively to film	Positive feedback	
4/29	Worked at assignment well	Positive feedback	
4/30	Participated in class No disruptions Left without signing	Called on her twice Positive feedback Recorded it	
5/1	Conference to discontinue anecdotal records		

Day 3
My second-period class was again very well behaved. I did, however, need to put a few negative remarks (for example, talking during film) on the anecdotal records. I will continue to keep close tabs on the situation.

Day 4
My second-period class (anecdotal records) is quickly becoming one of my best. We are covering more material, getting more class participation, and having less extraneous talking. I did need to make a couple of negative remarks on the record; but on seeing them, the students should, hopefully, maintain a positive attitude and appropriate behavior.

Teacher's Log—Eighth-Grade Science
Day 1
I discovered a method with which to deal with some major discipline problems in one of my classes. It uses an anecdotal record, which is a record of student actions and student behaviors. I think it will probably work because it holds the student accountable for her behaviors. If something must be done, the student has nobody to blame but herself.

Day 2
Today, I set up private conferences with anecdotal record students. I wonder if they'll show up—and if they do, how will they respond?

Day 3
Two students (of three) showed up for their anecdotal record conferences. The third is absent. Both students were very cooperative and made a commitment to better behavior. One student even made the comment that she thought this idea was a good one for her. The way things look, this will work out fairly well. We'll see . . .

Day 8
One of the students on anecdotal record has improved in behavior so much that I informed her that if her good behavior kept improving, I'd take her off the record next Wednesday. I think it will be interesting to see how her behavior will be; will it keep improving or will it backtrack again?

Implementing any new strategy may be difficult, and anecdotal record keeping is no exception. The teacher must expect that some students will be quite hostile when the procedure is introduced. Some may adamantly refuse to sign the record; others may scribble an unrecognizable signature. The teacher must remain calm and positive and simply record these behaviors. This action communicates to the student that she is solely responsible for her behavior and that the teacher is only an impartial recorder of the behavior. Student behavior will usually improve, given time. Since improved behavior becomes a part of the record, the anecdotal record reinforces the improvement and becomes the basis for a cycle of improvement.

When the student's behavior has improved to an acceptable level, the teacher informs that it will no longer be necessary to keep the anecdotal record because of the improvement in her behavior. It is important, as suggested earlier, to connect the improved behavior to academic success and improved grades if possible. It must also be made clear to the student that her fine behavior is expected to continue. Because continued attention is a key link in the chain of behaviors that turn disruptive students into students who behave appropriately, the teacher must continue to give the student attention when she behaves appropriately. If the student's behavior shows no improvement, it may be time to discontinue the process.

It can be quite difficult to decide when to stop recording behavior. There are no hard-and-fast rules, but there are some helpful guidelines. If the student has displayed acceptable behavior for a few days to a week, the record may be discontinued. If the student's behavior remains disruptive continuously for a week, the record keeping should be discontinued and the student told why. If the misbehavior is somewhat reduced, it may be advisable to have a second conference with the student to determine whether to continue record keeping.

Behavior Contracting

The third technique is behavior contracting. Behavior contracting is a teacher-directed strategy. This technique is grounded in the principles of operant conditioning, which state that a behavior that is reinforced is likely to be repeated and that a behavior that is not reinforced will disappear.

This technique involves the use of a written agreement, known as a behavior contract, between the teacher and student that commits the student to behave appropriately and offers a specified reward when the commitment is met. The contract details the expected behavior, a time period during which this behavior must be exhibited, and the reward that will be provided. The purposes of the contract are to manage behavior that is not managed by normal classroom procedures, to encourage self-discipline, and to foster the student's sense of commitment to appropriate classroom behavior. Although behavior contracting can be used with students at any grade level, it often is more appropriate and effective with elementary and middle school students since older students often resent the obvious attempt to manipulate their behavior. This technique is frequently and effectively used in special education classes.

Because an integral part of behavior contracting is the use of rewards, often extrinsic, concrete rewards, some teachers may be philosophically opposed to the technique. These teachers often overcome their philosophical objections by replacing concrete, extrinsic rewards with those more focused on learning activities, such as additional computer time, library passes, or assignment of special classroom duties and responsibilities. Teachers who feel that students should not be rewarded for behavior that is normally expected should keep in mind the fact that this technique has been shown to be effective and is one of the last possible strategies that can be used within the classroom. However, if there are strong philosophical objections to the technique, the teacher should not use it because the likelihood of its successful use is diminished if its philosophical underpinnings are in contradiction to the teacher's.

Teachers who decide to use behavior contracting should remember that it is unlikely that one contract will turn a chronically disruptive student into the epitome of model behavior. Usually the teacher must use a series of short-term behavior contracts that result in steady, gradual improvement in the student's behavior. A series of short-term behavior contracts allow the student to see the behavior changes as manageable and to receive small rewards after short intervals of improvement. In other words, a series of contracts provides the student with the opportunity to be successful. Manageable changes in behavior, shorter time intervals, and frequent opportunities for success make it more likely that the student will remain motivated.

In designing the series of contracts, the teacher should keep three principles in mind. First, design the contracts to require specific, gradual improvements in behavior. For example, if a student normally disrupts learning six times a period, set the initial goal at four disruptions or fewer per day. Over time increase the goal until it is set at zero disruptions per day. Second, gradually lengthen the time period during which the contract must be observed in order to gain the reward. For instance, the set time is one day for the first contract, a few days for the second contract, a week for the third contract, and so on. Third, move little by little from more tangible, extrinsic rewards to less tangible, more intrinsic rewards. Thus, a pencil or other supplies are the rewards under the first few contracts, and free time for pleasure reading is the reward under a later contract. Using these three principles takes advantage of a behavior modification technique called behavior shaping and gradually shifts management over the student's behavior from the teacher to the student, where it rightfully belongs.

Before writing the contract, the teacher should make a record of the student's past misbehaviors and the techniques that were used to try to ameliorate these misbehaviors. The teacher should use all available evidence, including documents and personal recollections, and try to be as accurate and neutral as possible. This record will help the teacher to decide which specific behaviors must be changed and how much change seems manageable for the student at one time. It also ensures that all appropriate management techniques have been used before the implementation of the behavior contract process. Once the record is compiled, the teacher holds a private conference with the student. It is best to begin the conference on a positive note. The teacher should communicate to the student that she has the potential to do well and to succeed if she can learn to behave appropriately. In doing this, the teacher is employing the concept of encouragement (Dreikurs, Grundwald, and Pepper, 1998). The teacher should then attempt to get the student to acknowledge that her behavior has been inappropriate and to recognize its negative impact on everyone in the classroom. Stressing the effect of the student's behavior on others promotes the development of higher moral reasoning (Tanner, 1978). To help the student recognize that her behavior has been unacceptable, the teacher may want to use questions similar to these: "What have you been doing in class?" "How is that affecting your chances of success?" "How would you like it if other students treated you like that?" "How would you like it if you were in a class you really liked but never got a chance to learn because other students were always causing trouble?" Thereafter, the teacher should tell the student that her behavior, no matter what the explanation for it, is unacceptable and must change. This is followed by a statement such as "I'd like to work out a plan with you that will help you to behave more appropriately in class."

The teacher must clearly state how the plan works. Because a contract is an agreement between two people, if the student refuses to make a commitment to the contract, the technique cannot be used. If, however, the student commits herself to improvements in classroom behavior for a specified period of time some positive consequences or rewards result. The reward may be free time for activities of special interest; a letter, note, or phone call to parents describing the improvements in behavior; or supplies, such as posters, pencils, and stickers, from the school bookstore. The most important consideration in deciding what particular reward to use is whether or not it is perceived as motivating by the student. For that reason, it is often a good idea to allow the student to suggest possible rewards or to discuss rewards with the student. If the student's parents are cooperative, it is sometimes possible to ask them to provide a reward at home that is meaningful to the student. At this point, the teacher should draw up the contract, setting forth the specific improvements in behavior, the time period, and the reward. The contract should then be signed by both the teacher and student and each should receive a copy. In the case of young students, it is often a good idea to send a copy of the contract home to parents as well. The conference should end as it began, on a positive note. The teacher, for example, might tell the student that she is looking forward to positive changes in the student's behavior.

Figure 7 is an example of a behavior contract and a behavior contract checklist that may be used by teachers to evaluate the quality of contracts that they draw up. The sample contract was the third in a series between Jessica and her fifth-grade teacher, Ms. Jones. Before the behavior contract intervention, Jessica spent the vast majority of each day's 40-minute social studies period wandering around the room. The first two contracts resulted in her being able to remain seated for about half the period.

Once the contract is made, the teacher should record the behavior of the student each day in regard to the terms specified in the contract. At the end of the contract period, the teacher can use this record to conduct a conference with the student. If the student has kept her commitment, the teacher should provide the reward. If the student's behavior needs further improvement, the teacher can draw up a new contract that specifies increased improvement over a longer time period. If at the end of the contract, the student's behavior has improved sufficiently to conform to final expectations, the teacher can inform the student that a behavior contract is no longer needed. If possible, the teacher should point out to the student the direct relationship between the improved behavior and the student's academic success in the classroom. The teacher also should make clear that she expects acceptable behavior and success to continue. Of course, the teacher must continue to give the student attention after the contract has ended. This consistent attention helps the student to recognize that positive behavior results in positive consequences and usually helps to maintain appropriate behavior over a long period of time.

If at the end of the contract period the student has not kept the commitment, the teacher should accept no excuses. During the conference, the teacher should assume a neutral role, explaining that the reward cannot be given because the student's behavior did not live up to the behavior specified in the contract. The teacher should point out to the student that the lack of reward is simply a logical consequence of the behavior. This helps the student to see the cause-and-effect relationship between behavior and its consequences. If the student learns only this, she has learned an extremely valuable lesson.

At this point, the teacher must decide whether or not it is worth trying a new contract with the student. If the teacher believes that the student tried to live up to the contract, a new contract that calls for a little less drastic improvement or calls for improvement over a slightly shorter time frame may be worthwhile.

If the student has not made a sincere effort to improve, obviously the contracting is not working. It is time to try another option. Nothing has been lost in the attempt except a little bit of time, and the teacher has accumulated additional documentation, which will be helpful if it is necessary to seek outside assistance.

There is one final technique for the teacher to try when these classroom management techniques do not work. This is the exclusion of the student from the classroom until she makes a written commitment to improve her behavior.

Prior to exclusion, the teacher tells the student that she is no longer welcome in the class because of her disruptive behavior, which is interfering with the teacher's right to teach and the students' right to learn. The teacher then tells the student to report to a specified location in the school where appropriate classroom assignments involving reading and writing will be given. The student is also told that she will be held accountable for the completion of all assignments in an acceptable and timely manner, the same as required in the regular classroom. The teacher stresses that the student may return to the classroom at any time by giving a written commitment to improve her behavior. This written commitment must be in the student's own words and must specify the changed behavior that will be evident when the student returns to the classroom. Of course, exclusion presupposes that the administration is supportive of such a technique and has made appropriate arrangements for the setting.

Our experience has shown that those few students who have been excluded from the classroom and have then made the written commitment and returned have remained in the classroom with acceptable behavior. Exclusion finally demonstrates to the student that her behavior will no longer be tolerated and that the entire responsibility for the student's behavior is on the student and only the student.

If a student does not make the written commitment within a reasonable period of time, usually no more than a few days, outside assistance (in the form of parents, counselor, principal, or outside agency) must be sought. If it is necessary to seek outside assistance, the teacher's use of self-monitoring, anecdotal record keeping, or behavior contracting will provide the documented evidence needed to make an appropriate referral.

FIGURE 7 *Third Contract between Jessica and Ms. Jones*

1. *Expected Behavior*
   Jessica remains in her seat for the first 30 minutes of each social studies period.

2. *Time Period*
   Monday, February 27, to Friday, March 3.

3. *Reward*
   If Jessica remains in her seat for the first 30 minutes of each social studies period,
   a. she can choose the class's outdoor game on Friday afternoon, March 3.
   b. Ms. Jones will telephone her parents to tell them of the improvement in Jessica's behavior on Friday afternoon, March 3.

4. *Evaluation*
   a. After each social studies period, Ms. Jones records whether Jessica did or did not get out of her seat during the first 30 minutes.
   b. Jessica and Ms. Jones will meet on Friday, March 3, at 12:30 PM to determine whether the contract has been performed and write next week's fourth contract.

Student _____

Teacher _____

Date _____

Behavior Contract Checklist

1. Is the expected behavior described specifically? _____ Yes _____No
2. Is the time period specified clearly? _____ Yes _____No
3. Has the reward been specified clearly? _____ Yes _____No
4. Is the reward motivating to the student? _____ Yes _____No
5. Is the evaluation procedure specified? _____ Yes _____No
6. Has a date been set to meet to review the contract? _____ Yes _____No
7. Has the student understood, agreed to, and signed the contract? _____ Yes _____No
8. Has the teacher signed the contract? _____ Yes _____No
9. Do both the teacher and student have copies? _____ Yes _____No
10. Did the student's parents get a copy of the contract? _____ Yes _____No

REFERENCES

Abi-Nader, J. (1993). Meeting the needs of multicultural classrooms: Family values and the motivation of minority students. In M. J. O'Hair and S. J. Odell (Eds.), *Diversity and Teaching: Teacher Education Yearbook 1.*Fort Worth, TX: Harcourt, Brace, Jovanovich College Publications.

Ames, R., and Ames, C. (Eds.). (1984). *Research on Motivation in Education,* Vol. 1: *Student Motivation.* New York: Academic.

Bandura, A. (1977). *Social Learning Theory.* Englewood Cliffs, NJ: Prentice Hall.

Bandura, A. (1986). *Social Foundations of Thought and Action: Social Cognition Theory.* Englewood Cliffs, NJ: Prentice Hall.

Brendtro, L. K., Brokenleg, M., and Van Bockern, S. (1990). *Reclaiming Youth at Risk: Our Hope for the Future.* Bloomington, IN: National Educational Service.

Brophy, J. E. (1987). Synthesis of research strategies on motivating students to learn. *Educational Leadership, 45, 2,* 40-48.

Brophy, J. E. (1988a). Educating teachers about managing classrooms and students. *Teaching and Teacher Education, 4,* 1, 1-18.

Brophy, J. E. (1988b). Research on teacher effects and abuses. *Elementary School Journal, 89,* 1, 3-21.

Canter, L. (1989). Assertive Discipline—More than names on the board and marbles in a jar. *Phi Delta Kappan, 71,* 1, 57-61.

Canter, L., and Canter, M. (1992). *Assertive Discipline: Positive Behavior Management for Today's Classrooms,* rev. ed., Santa Monica, CA: Canter Associates.

Curwin, R. L., and Mendler, A. N. (1980). *The Discipline Book: A Complete Guide to School and Classroom Management.* Reston, VA: Reston Publishing.

Dreikurs, R. (1964). *Children the Challenge.* New York: Hawthorne.

Dreikurs, R., Grundwald, B. B., and Pepper, F. C. (1998). *Maintaining Sanity in the Classroom: Classroom Management Techniques,* 2nd ed. New York: Harper & Row.

Emmer, E. T., Evertson, C. M., Sanford, J. P., Clements, B. S., and Worsham, M. E. (1989). *Classroom Management for Secondary Teachers,* 2nd ed. Englewood Cliffs, NJ: Prentice Hall.

Emmer, E. T., Evertson, C. M., Sanford, J. P., Clements, B. S., and Worsham, M. E. (1997). *Classroom Management for Secondary Teachers,* 4th ed. Boston: Allyn and Bacon.

Evertson, C. M., and Emmer, E. T. (1982). Preventive classroom management. In D. L. Duke (Ed.), *Helping Teachers Manage Classrooms,* pp. 2-31. Alexandria, VA: Association for Supervision and Curriculum Development.

Feathers, N. (1982). *Expectations and Actions.* Hillsdale, NJ: Erlbaum.

Feldhusen, J. F. (1978). Behavior problems in secondary schools. *Journal of Research and Development in Education, 11,* 4, 17-28.

Ginott, H. (1972). *Between Teacher and Child.* New York: Peter H. Wyden.

Glasser, W. (1969). *Schools Without Failure.* New York: Harper & Row.

Good, T., and Brophy, J. (1997). *Looking in Classrooms,* 4th ed. New York: Harper & Row.

Gordon, T. (1989). *Teaching Children Self-Discipline at Home and in School.* New York: Random House.

Hunter, M. (1982). *Mastery Teaching.* El Segundo, CA: TIP Publications.

Irvine, J. J. (1990). *Black Students and School Failure: Policy, Practices, Prescriptions.* Westport, CT: Greenwood.

Johnson, S. M., Boadstad, D. D., and Lobitz, G. K. (1976). Generalization and contrast phenomena in behavior modification with children. In E. J. Mash, L. A. Hamerlynck, and L. C. Handy (Eds.), *Behavior Modification and Families.* New York: Brunner/Mazell.

Johnson, D. W., Johnson, R. T., and Holubec, E. J. (1993). *Cooperation in the Classroom,* 6th ed. Edina, MN: Interaction Book Company.

Jones, V. F. (1980). *Adolescents with Behavior Problems.* Boston: Allyn and Bacon.

Jones, V. F., and Jones, L. S. (1998). *Comprehensive Classroom Management: Creating Positive Learning Environments and Solving Problems,* 5th ed. Boston: Allyn and Bacon.

Kindsvatter, R. (1978). A new view of the dynamics of discipline. *Phi Delta Kappan, 59,* 5, 322-365.

Kochman, T. (1981). *Black and White: Styles in Conflict.* Chicago: University of Chicago Press.

Ladson-Billings, G. (1994). *The Dreamkeepers: Successful Teachers of African American Children.* San Francisco: Jossey Bass.

Lasley, T. J. (1989). A teacher development model for classroom management. *Phi Delta Kappan, 71,* 1, 36-38.

Levin, J., Nolan, J., and Hoffman, N. (1985) A strategy for the classroom resolution of chronic discipline problems. *National Association of Secondary School Principals Bulletin, 69,* 7, 11-18.

Redl, F., and Wineman, D. (1952). *Controls from Within.* New York: Free Press.

Rinne, C. (1984). *Attention: The Fundamentals of Classroom Control.* Columbus, OH: Merrill.

Rosenshine, B., and Stevens, R. (1986). Teaching functions. In M. C. Wittrock (Ed.), *Handbook of Research on Teaching,* 3rd ed. New York: Macmillan.

Saphier, J., and Gower, R. (1982). *The Skillful Teacher.* Carlisle, MA: Research for Better Teaching.

Shrigley, R. L. (1979). Strategies in classroom management. *The National Association of Secondary School Principals Bulletin, 63,* 428, 1-9.

Shrigley, R. L. (1985). Curbing student disruption in the classroom—Teachers need intervention skills. *National Association of Secondary School Principals Bulletin, 69,* 479, 26-32.

Stipek, D. (1993). *Motivation to Learn: From Theory to Practice,* 2nd ed. Boston: Allyn and Bacon.

Stipek, D. J. (1998). *Motivation to Learn: From Theory to Practice,* 3rd ed. Boston: Allyn and Bacon.

Strachota, R. (1996). *On Their Side: Helping Children Take Charge of Their Learning.* Greenfield, MA: Northeast Foundation for Children.

Tanner, L. N. (1978). *Classroom Discipline for Effective Teaching and Learning.* New York: Holt, Rinehart, & Winston.

Walker, H. M. (1979). *The Acting-Out Child: Coping with Classroom Disruption.* Boston: Allyn and Bacon.

Wang, M. C., and Palinscar, A. S. (1989). Teaching students to assume an active role in their learning. In M. C. Reynolds (Ed.), *Knowledge Base for the Beginning Teacher.* New York: Pergamon.

Weiner, B. (1980). A cognitive (attribution)—emotion—action, model of motivated behavior: An analysis of judgments of help-giving. *Journal of Personality and Social Psychology, 39,* 186-200.